A Global Foods Tour

Glencoe McGraw-Hill

New York, New York   Columbus, Ohio   Woodland Hills, California   Peoria, Illinois

To the Teacher

A Global Foods Tour is a complete curriculum that can be use on its own or as an extension of a separate foods program. To allow maximum teaching-plan flexibility, this book is divided into three parts:

Part 1: Global Foods: An overview for teaching suggestions, suggested student objectives, suggested resources, activities, and student project worksheets that will help you incorporate the study of global foods into your curriculum. The materials in this section can be used alone or with Part 2.

Part 2: A Global Foods Tour: A collection of student learning materials that will take students on an imaginary Global Foods Tour that includes 11 regional overviews and features 25 ports of call. A portfolio of 12 maps and a total of 49 recipes representing the regions visited round out these materials. For a more detailed overview of this section, see pages 14 and 15.

Part 3: Global Awareness: Teaching suggestions, suggested student objectives, suggested resources, activities, student handouts, and student project worksheets. The materials in this section help raise students' awareness of both world interdependence and the unequal distribution of the world's resources.

Design and production assistance provided by
Howard Portnoy Editorial Services

Glencoe/McGraw-Hill
A Division of The McGraw-Hill Companies

Send all inquiries to:

Glencoe/McGraw-Hill
3008 W. Willow Knolls Drive
Peoria, Illinois 61614-1083

ISBN 0-07-820699-5

Printed in the United States of America

3 4 5 6 7 8 9 10   009   04 03 02 01 00

TABLE OF CONTENTS

Part 3: Global Awareness

Teaching Global Foods

North America has always been home to members of diverse cultures, from the many Native American tribes who were the original inhabitants to the waves of immigrants who settled into a new life here. According to the U.S. Bureau of the Census, in 1995 there were an estimated 23 million foreign-born persons living in the United States. That number represents nearly 1 in every 11 Americans.

Most teachers need look no further for evidence of cultural diversity than their own classrooms. The students in today's classrooms represent an ever-widening range of cultural and ethnic groups. Many students, and an even greater number of parents, were born outside the United States.

Today's culturally diverse population lends urgency to the need for students to respect and appreciate cultural diversity. The first step toward developing respect and appreciation is understanding. Teachers can help their students begin to understand cultures different from their own on several fronts. Certainly teachers will want to draw on community members as resources. Exchange students, owners of ethnic restaurants, or anyone with roots in another culture might be willing to serve as guest speakers or simply to provide information. One of the most successful and enjoyable ways to promote understanding is to expose students to the foods and food customs of various cultures.

People of different cultures may enjoy one another's foods even if their customs, beliefs, and political views clash. Because food choices are among the first cultural elements to be accepted by other cultures, the study of foods can help further students' appreciation of cultural diversity.

The benefits of studying global foods include the following:

◆ Broadens students' horizons, encouraging them to try new foods and vary their food choices.
◆ Helps clear up misconceptions or negative feelings they may have about other cultures.
◆ Provides positive associations with people of other cultures.
◆ Adds interest to lessons and motivates students to learn more about foods and nutrition in general.

Modern transportation and growing global trade increase the likelihood that today's students will, at some time in their lives, visit or live in another country. Even without leaving the United States, they may, now or in the future, have occasion to share meals with people of other cultures. A knowledge of world foods and food customs can prepare students for these experiences.

Suggested Objectives

As part of a course or unit on global foods, students may be asked to:

◆ Compare the ways people of different cultures meet their basic nutrient needs.
◆ Explain why and how certain foods have become staples in a given country.
◆ Identify factors that influence food choices and customs.
◆ Identify foods of different cultures and describe their history.
◆ Describe the role of food in traditional celebrations around the world.
◆ Trace the development of food traditions in the United States.
◆ Prepare dishes characteristic of various cultures.

Suggested References for Teaching Global Foods

Books

Anderson, E. N. *Food of China*. New Haven, Conn.: Yale University Press, 1990.

Anderson, Jean. *Food of Portugal*. New York: Hearst Books, 1994.

Barron, Rosemary. *Flavors of Greece*. New York: Morrow, 1991.

Belleme, Jan, and John Belleme. *Cooking with Japanese Foods*. Garden City Park, N.Y.: Avery Publishing, 1993.

Biro, Charlotte S. *Flavors of Hungary*. Santa Rosa, Calif.: Cole Group, 1992.

Child, Julia. *The French Chef Cookbook*. New York: Bantam, 1982.

Esposito, Mary Ann. *Ciao Italia*. New York: Hearst Books, 1991.

Farah, Madelain. *Lebanese Cuisine*. Portland, Ore.: Lebanese Cuisine, 1985.

Garmey, Jane. *Great British Cooking: A Well-Kept Secret*. New York: Harper Collins, 1992.

Harris, Dunstan A. *Island Cooking: Recipes from the Caribbean*. Freedom, Calif.: Crossing Press, 1988.

Harris, Jessica B. *Tasting Brazil*. New York: Macmillan, 1992.

Hutton, Wendy. *Food of Thailand: Authentic Recipes from the Golden Kingdom*. Berkeley, Calif.: Periplus, 1994.

Irwin, Florence. *Cookin' Woman: Irish Country Recipes*. Chester Springs, Pa.: Dufour Editions, 1992.

Keao, Mae, and Lee Keao. *Cooking With Hawaiian Magic*. Honolulu: Bess Press, 1990.

Lund, Duane R. *Scandinavian Cookbook*. Cambridge, Minn.: Adventure Publications, 1992.

Marden, Patricia, and Suzanne Barchers. *Cooking Up World History: Multicultural Recipes and Resources*. Englewood, Colo.: Teacher Ideas Press, 1994.

Mazda, Maideh. *In a Persian Kitchen*. Boston: Charles E. Tuttle, 1960.

Millon, Marc, and Kim Millon. *Flavours of Korea*. North Pomfret, Vt.: Trafalgar, 1991.

Ngo, Bach, and Gloria Zimmerman. *Classic Cuisine of Vietnam*. New York: NAL-Dutton, 1986.

Ortiz, Elisabeth L. *The Book of Latin American Cooking*. Hopewell, N.J.: Ecco Press, 1994.

Petrovskaya, Kyra. *Russian Cookbook*. New York: Dover, 1992.

Rebarto, Manuel. *Spanish Cooking*. Edison, N.J.: Book Sales, Inc., 1993.

Revel, Jean-Francois. *Culture and Cuisine*. New York: Da Capo, 1984.

Rozin, Elisabeth. *Ethnic Cuisine: Authentic Flavors of 30 International Cuisines*. New York: Viking Penguin, 1992.

Sandler, Bea. *African Cookbook*. New York: Carol Publishing Group, 1993.

Scharfenberg, Horst. *The Cuisines of Germany*. New York: Poseidon Press, 1989.

Slebsager, Astrid. *Cooking with the Danes*. Vero Beach, Fla.: Arthur Vanous Co., 1991.

Spieler, Marlena. *Flavors of Mexico: Fresh, Simple Twists on Classic Regional Dishes*. Los Angeles: Lowell House, 1991.

(Continued on next page)

Internet

> **Internet Disclaimer**
>
> The Internet listings referenced in this book are a source for extended information related to the text. We have made every effort to recommend sites that are informative and accurate. However, these sites are not under the control of Glencoe/McGraw-Hill, and, therefore, Glencoe/McGraw-Hill makes no representation concerning the content of these sites. We strongly encourage teachers to preview sites before students use them. Many sites may eventually contain "hot links" to other sites that could lead to exposure to inappropriate material. Internet sites are sometimes "under construction" and may not always be available. Sites may also move or have been discontinued completely by the time you or your students attempt to access them.

FYNet's Malaysian Recipe site – links to collections of Malaysian recipes
http://ucsee.eecs.berkeley.edu/~soh/recipe.html

Hawaiian Electric Co.'s "Electric Kitchen" – Hawaiian, Portuguese, and Puerto Rican recipes
http://www.hei.com/heco/ekitchen/ekitchen.html

La Cocina Mexicana – collection of Mexican menus and recipes
http://mexico.udg.mx/Cocina/ingles/

La Cocina Venezolana – collection of Venezuelan recipes
http://members.tripod.com/~cocinavzla/

Manong Ken's Filipino Eatery on the Internet – recipes and information on Filipino cuisine
http://www.tribo.org/food.html

Pedro's Kitchen – Brazilian recipes, links to related sites, and information about Brazil
http://www.toucansolutions.com/pedro/

Prapapun's Hobby Kitchen – collection of Thai recipes
http://www.gezi.com:80/gzworld/recipe/index.html

Stuart's Chinese Recipes – collection of Chinese recipes
http://www.dcs.gla.ac.uk/~blairsa/Chinese_Recipes.html

Turkish Cuisine – collection of Turkish recipes
http://www.cs.umd.edu/users/kandogan/FTA/TurkishCuisine/cuisine.html

Activities and Projects for Teaching Global Foods

Please note: These projects and activities may be used independently, or incorporated into the activities in **A Global Foods Tour,** *which begin on page 14. For some activities, specific possible ties to* **A Global Foods Tour** *are indicated in parentheses.*

Foreign Meal Patterns. Have students prepare and serve high tea (United Kingdom), Merienda (Mexico), or some other meal traditional in another culture and not usually served in the United States.

Dietary Laws Guest Speaker. (South Asia; Southwest Asia and North Africa) Invite a Jewish, Islamic, or Hindu religious spokesperson to speak about dietary laws in his or her religion. Ask him or her to discuss food preparation as well as the foods themselves.

Menu Planning. (South Asia; Southwest Asia and North Africa) Tell students to imagine they are hosting a reception that will be attended by members of Orthodox Judaic, Islamic, and Hindu religions. Have them research dietary laws for the three religions and then work in groups to prepare a list of hors d'oeuvres that all guests can eat.

Spice Research. (East and Southeast Asia) Have interested students research the role of spices during the Age of Exploration (1400s to 1800s). Allow them to share their findings with the class. Follow up by discussing how spices are used today.

Guest Speaker. Invite a native of another country, the chef or owner of an ethnic restaurant, a participant in an exchange program, or another qualified person to speak to your class about the food customs of the culture he or she represents.

Food Customs and Prejudices. Have students imagine themselves travelers on a global foods tour. Ask them to research and list foods they might be served in various countries that might clash with their food preferences and have them consider and discuss how they might handle such a situation. Have them guess foods commonly served in the United States that visitors from certain other countries might find unusual.

Etiquette of Other Lands. Have students research and list facts about food-related etiquette in various cultures that might be useful for people who work abroad. What foods are eaten with fingers in various countries? Where, for example, is it unacceptable to eat with the left hand?

World Holidays. Keep track of traditional holidays around the world. Observe the holidays in class by having small groups of students prepare and serve traditional dishes.

Healthful Menu Project. Reproduce and distribute **Global Foods Project 1, "Healthful Ethnic Menu"** (page 10). To help students plan an ethnic menu that fits the Dietary Guidelines for Americans and the Food Guide Pyramid, have them complete the project as directed.

Special Occasion Project. Reproduce and distribute **Global Foods Project 2, "Food Customs for a Special Occasion"** (page 11). To help students explore food traditions surrounding a holiday in another culture, have them complete the project as directed.

International Foods Day Project. This project is an excellent way to close students work on the activities in *A Global Foods Tour.* Reproduce and distribute **Global Foods Project 3, "International Foods Day"** (page 12). Have students complete the project as directed. To enhance their appreciation for cuisines of other cultures, help them conduct an international fair where participants can sample foods from many parts of the world. Teachers should be prepared to take an active role in planning and carrying out this project.

Global Foods Project 1

Healthful Ethnic Menu

The Dietary Guidelines for Americans can be met by people with various eating patterns and food preferences. To expand your eating experiences while keeping within healthy limits, observe the Dietary Guidelines while enjoying the cuisines of many cultures.

Purpose

To plan an ethnic menu choosing foods that meet the Dietary Guidelines for Americans

Resources

◆ Ethnic cookbooks

◆ Dietary Guidelines for Americans

◆ Food Guide Pyramid

Materials

◆ Graph paper

Procedure

1. Choose a country with a cuisine different from your usual food pattern. Research the meal patterns and foods commonly eaten in that country.

2. Plan and write out menus for one day that reflect the meal patterns and cuisine of your chosen country. Be sure the day's

choices supply the recommended number of servings from each of the five food groups. (One dish may provide servings from several food groups.)

3. Obtain recipes for the foods listed on your menus, if possible.

4. Review your menus and recipes. Be sure they follow the Dietary Guidelines. Overall, are your menus likely to be low in fat, saturated fat, cholesterol, sugar, and sodium? If not, make needed changes by modifying recipes or substituting different menu items.

5. When you are satisfied with your menus, prepare a report that includes the following:

◆ A listing of the menus you planned.

◆ An explanation of why the meals you planned are typical of the country you chose.

◆ A graph showing how your menus supply the recommended number of servings from each food group.

◆ An explanation of why you feel your menu is in keeping with the Dietary Guidelines for Americans.

◆ The recipes you have chosen, including any modifications you made and an explanation for those changes.

Global Foods Project 2

Food Customs for a Special Occasion

One way cultures retain their unique identities is through their celebration of special occasions. Customs surrounding special occasions have often been handed down for hundreds of years. Learning about these customs is an interesting way to gain an appreciation of another culture.

Purpose

To study the food traditions surrounding a holiday in a specific culture other than your own.

Resources

◆ Books (including textbooks) and periodicals that focus on foods used in celebrations

◆ Internet and other information sources that focus on foods used in celebrations

◆ Ethnic cookbooks

◆ Community resources (restaurants, cultural centers, churches, individuals)

Materials

◆ Recipe ingredients and food preparation equipment

◆ Tables and chairs

◆ Serving and eating dishes and utensils

◆ Other materials as required for your group's presentation

Procedure

1. Work in groups as instructed by your teacher.

2. Choose a traditional holiday, feast, or celebration characteristic of a specific culture. The culture may be from another country or from the United States, as long as it is not one to which members of your group belong or are familiar with. You may choose a holiday that is observed in many parts of the world or a celebration that is unique to one area.

3. Research the history of the celebration and the way it is observed in that culture.

4. Research the dishes traditionally served on that occasion in the culture you have chosen. Select at least one recipe that you will prepare and serve to the class.

5. Research relevant customs for serving and eating food in the culture you have chosen.

6. If you wish, plan some traditional activities, such as music or dances, that accompany the celebration of the holiday you have chosen.

7. Prepare the recipe that your group selected.

8. Make a presentation to the class, explaining the holiday, its history, and the traditions surrounding it. Include any appropriate activities you wish. Serve the prepared dish to the class.

Global Foods Project 3

International Foods Day

An international foods day, whether it be a classroom event, a school lunchtime program, or a community fair, can provide opportunities to prepare and sample representative dishes from all over the world.

Purpose

To prepare and sample foods from many parts of the world.

Resources

◆ Internet and other information sources that focus on ethnic foods

◆ Ethnic cookbooks

◆ Community resources (restaurants, cultural centers, churches, individuals)

Materials

◆ Recipe ingredients and food preparation equipment

◆ Tables and chairs

◆ Serving and eating dishes and utensils

◆ Poster board

◆ Markers

◆ Labels

◆ Other materials depending on project

Procedure

1. As a class, decide on the scope of your project. Will you invite other students in your school, grade school students, or members of your community to attend? What will the project include? Here are some possibilities:

   ◆ Booths serving food from different countries

   ◆ Music playing at each booth

   ◆ Servers wearing native costumes

   ◆ Posters and other decorations

   ◆ Demonstrations and activities, such as folk dances and crafts

2. With your teacher's help, set a date, time, and location for your event. Allow at least a month to get ready. The larger the event, the more time you will need to plan and prepare.

3. Form committees that will prepare the presentation for each of the countries that will be represented. Form other committees to handle overall tasks such as advertising, arranging for the space, and so forth.

4. As class, make a list of what needs to be done. Assign one or more people to each task. Set a schedule so that everything will get done on time. Your list may include the following:

Responsibilities for committees handling countries

◆ Research foods and find recipes

◆ Work on other aspects of the event—costumes, music, entertainment, and decorations

◆ Obtain needed food preparation and serving equipment

◆ Make a shopping list and purchase ingredients

◆ Prepare foods

◆ Serve foods at the booth

◆ Clean up

Responsibilities for committees handling overall tasks

◆ Set a budget

◆ Advertise the event

◆ Gather equipment such as tables and chairs

(Continued on next page)

- ◆ Keep a list of borrowed items and label each item with the owner's name

- ◆ Set up booths

- ◆ Tear down booths and clean up after the event

- ◆ Return borrowed items

- ◆ Write thank-you notes

5. Contact people in the community for help. For example, perhaps local ethnic restaurants will donate some food or recipes. Embassies and tourist bureaus may be able to help with ideas or posters. Foreign language and social studies teachers may be able to offer ideas.

6. Have a booth for each country represented. Include a poster with the name of the country and a list of the dishes being served. Have a label for each type of food so the people who visit the booth can identify the different dishes.

7. When preparing and serving the foods, remember to follow proper sanitation procedures. Be sure you have a way to keep hot foods hot and cold foods cold.

8. Enjoy!

Teaching A Global Foods Tour

Materials

Pages 15 through 146 of this book are a collection of student learning materials to assist you in taking students on an imaginary global foods tour. The materials supplied are:

1. Traveler's Guide: An introduction of the idea of A Global Foods Tour.

2. Map Portfolio: A collection of 12 maps that help students locate each region on their tour and reinforce their general knowledge of geography.

3. Recipes, Recipe Worksheet, and Recipe Index: Each regional section of the tour includes recipes that represent cuisines from that region. There are a total of 49 recipes. A Global Foods Tour Recipe Index on pages 28 and 29 lists all 49 recipes organized into food categories. A Recipe Worksheet is provided on page 30 to help students plan, analyze, and evaluate the dishes they prepare.

4. The Tour Regions: The tour has been divided into 11 regions. You may wish to use the following list to plan which regions you will teach and the dates you will devote to each.

—- Touring the U.S.A
   —- Port of Call: Northeastern Region
   —- Port of Call: Southern Region
   —- Port of Call: Pacific Coast Region
   —- Port of Call: Midwestern Region
   —- Port of Call: Northwestern and South-western Region
—- Touring Canada
   —- Port of Call: Quebec
   —- Port of Call: British Columbia
—- Touring Latin America
   —- Port of Call: Puerto Rico
   —- Port of Call: Mexico
—- Touring Southern Europe
   —- Port of Call: Spain
   —- Port of Call: France
—- Touring Northern Europe
   —- Port of Call: United Kingdom
   —- Port of Call: Germany

—-Touring Eastern Europe and Northern Asia
   —- Port of Call: Russia
   —- Port of Call: Greece
—- Touring East and Southeast Asia
   —- Port of Call: Japan
   —- Port of Call: Vietnam
—- Touring South Asia
   —- Port of Call: India
   —- Port of Call: Sri Lanka
—- Touring Southwest Asia and North Africa
   —- Port of Call: Egypt
   —- Port of Call: Israel
—- Touring Africa South of the Sahara
   —- Port of Call: South Africa
   —- Port of Call: Kenya
—- Touring Australia and Oceania
   —- Port of Call: Australia
   —- Port of Call: New Zealand

Teaching Strategies

You may wish to enrich students' study of each region by incorporating into your lesson plans films, videos, and computer software that offer information on that region. Make use of all community resources including guest speakers with a connection to the regions studied.

Consider having students keep **A Global Foods Tour** scrapbook or travel journal to organize the information about each region they study.

Allow plenty of time for students to try some of the recipes for each region. You may wish to have teams of students prepare different recipes to allow everyone to experience as many ethnic dishes as possible.

A Global Foods Tour

Traveler's Guide

Some travel service companies plan and arrange foods tours for people who have a particular interest in foods and cuisine. The focus of a foods tours is, of course, food, but travelers on such a tour do more than visit restaurants and sample regional cuisine. Foods-tour travelers also learn about the geographical and cultural factors that influence the kinds of foods grown and eaten in each region that they visit. Foods-tour travelers usually sample the language of a region as they sample the food, often learning new names for familiar foods. Foods-tour travelers come away from their journey with a broadened view of the world, a deeper understanding of other cultures, and a growing appreciation of ethnic cuisine. Every foods-tour traveler also returns with a collection of recipes from the regions visited.

If the idea of a foods tour has your mouth watering, get ready to travel. You will have an opportunity to "visit" some or all of the following regions as you make your way around the globe on this tour of the world's foods.

- **Touring the U.S.A**
  Port of Call: Northeastern Region
  Port of Call: Southern Region
  Port of Call: Pacific Coast Region
  Port of Call: Midwestern Region
  Port of Call: Northwestern and Southwestern Region

- **Touring Canada**
  Port of Call: Quebec
  Port of Call: British Columbia

- **Touring Latin America**
  Port of Call: Puerto Rico
  Port of Call: Mexico

- **Touring Southern Europe**
  Port of Call: Spain
  Port of Call: France

- **Touring Northern Europe**
  Port of Call: United Kingdom
  Port of Call: Germany

- **Touring Eastern Europe and Northern Asia**
  Port of Call: Russia
  Port of Call: Greece

- **Touring East and Southeast Asia**
  Port of Call: Japan
  Port of Call: Vietnam

- **Touring South Asia**
  Port of Call: India
  Port of Call: Sri Lanka

- **Touring Southwest Asia and North Africa**
  Port of Call: Egypt
  Port of Call: Israel

- **Touring Africa South of the Sahara**
  Port of Call: South Africa
  Port of Call: Kenya

- **Touring Australia and Oceania**
  Port of Call: Australia
  Port of Call: New Zealand

The success of your imaginary foods tour, like the success of an actual tour, depends very much on the efforts you make to take advantage of the opportunities to learn about and experience a region and its cuisine. To make the most of your tour, look for newspaper and magazine articles about the regions your class plans to "visit." Read the articles and share the information with your classmates. Check the library for available travel films about the region that you can view and look for regional cookbooks to study. Do what you can to "be there!"

Enjoy!

A Global Foods Tour Map Portfolio

Map 1
The World

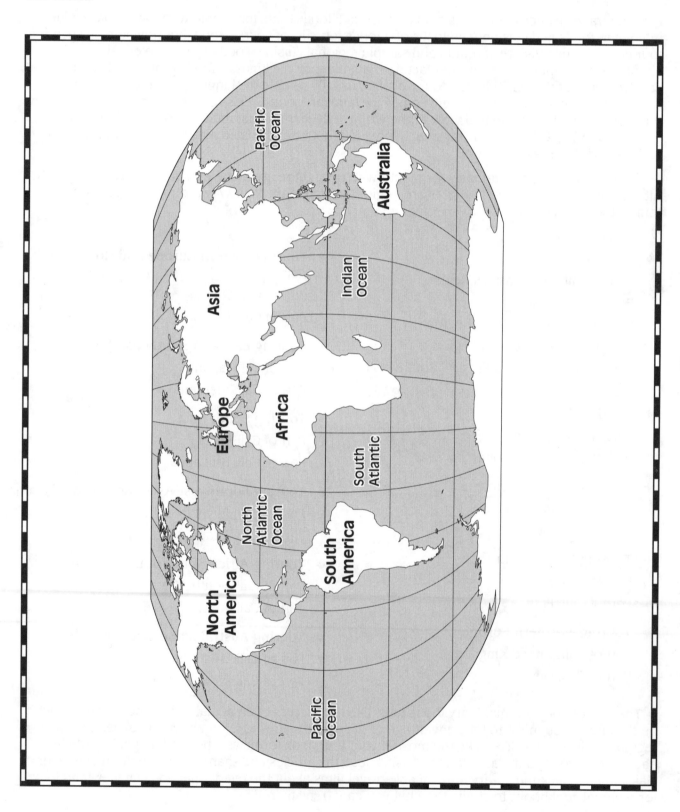

A Global Foods Tour Map Portfolio

Map 2
United States

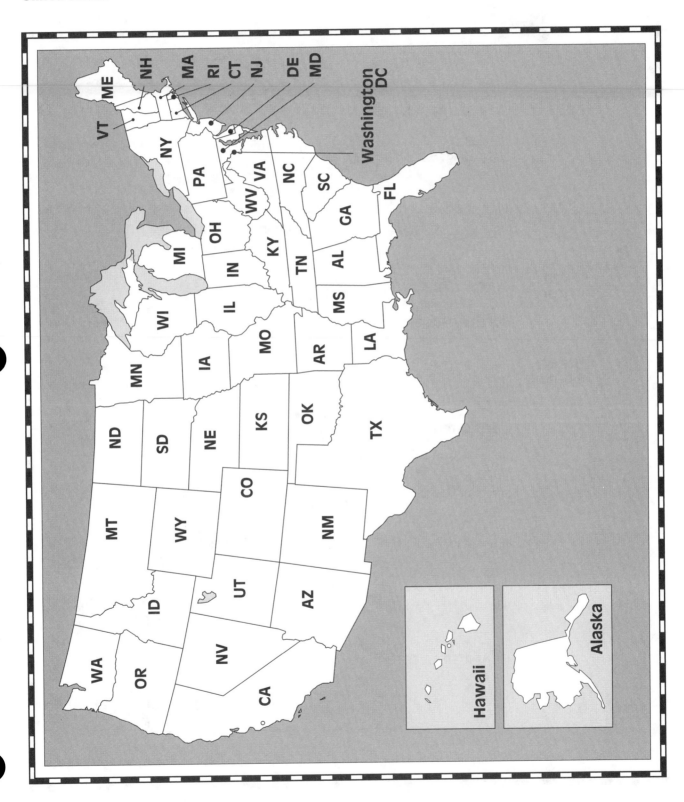

A Global Foods Tour Map Portfolio

Map 3
Canada

A Global Foods Tour Map Portfolio

Map 4
Latin America: Mexico, Central America, Caribbean

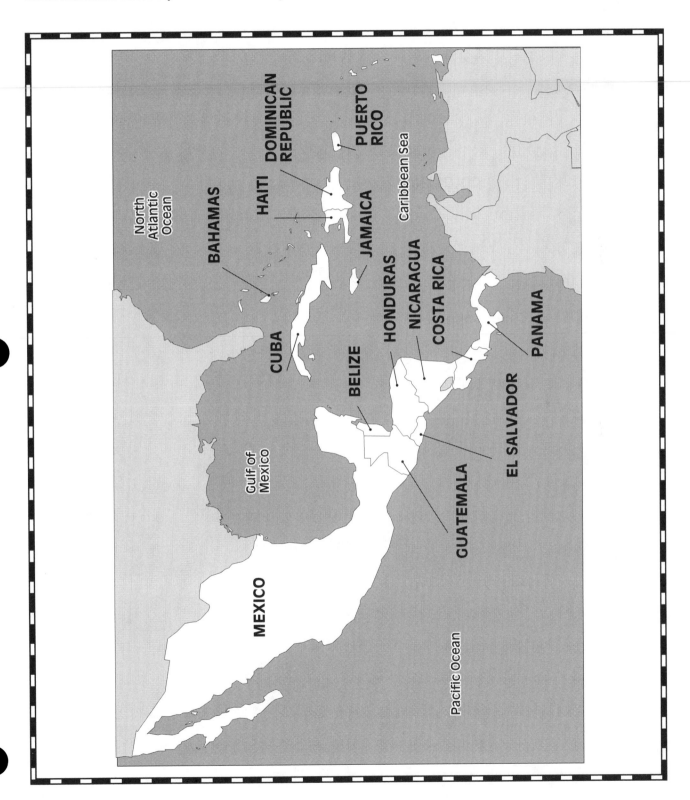

Name _____ Date _____ Class _____

A Global Foods Tour Map Portfolio

Map 5

Latin America: South America

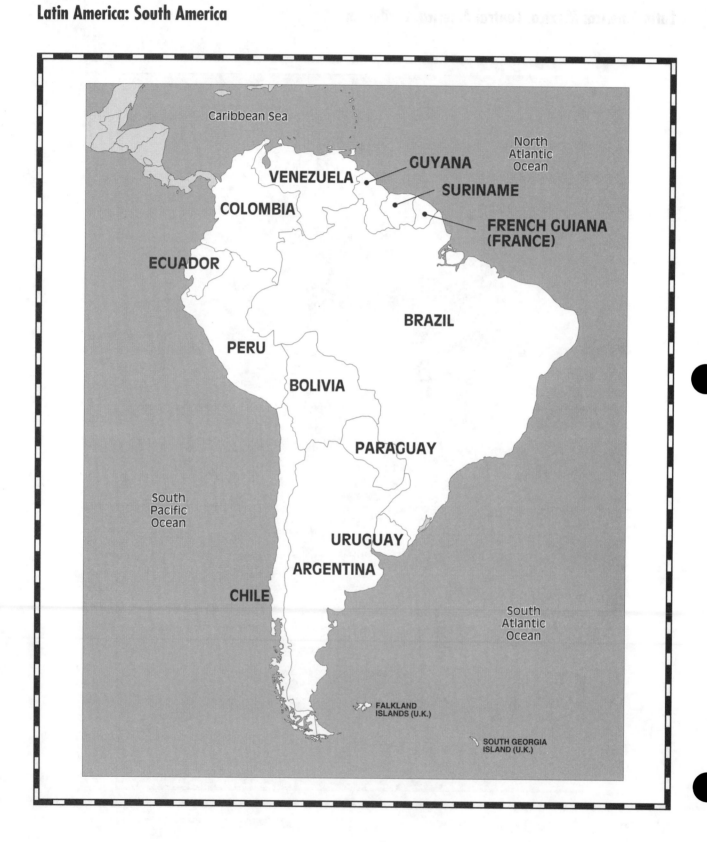

A Global Foods Tour Map Portfolio

Map 6
Northern and Southern Europe

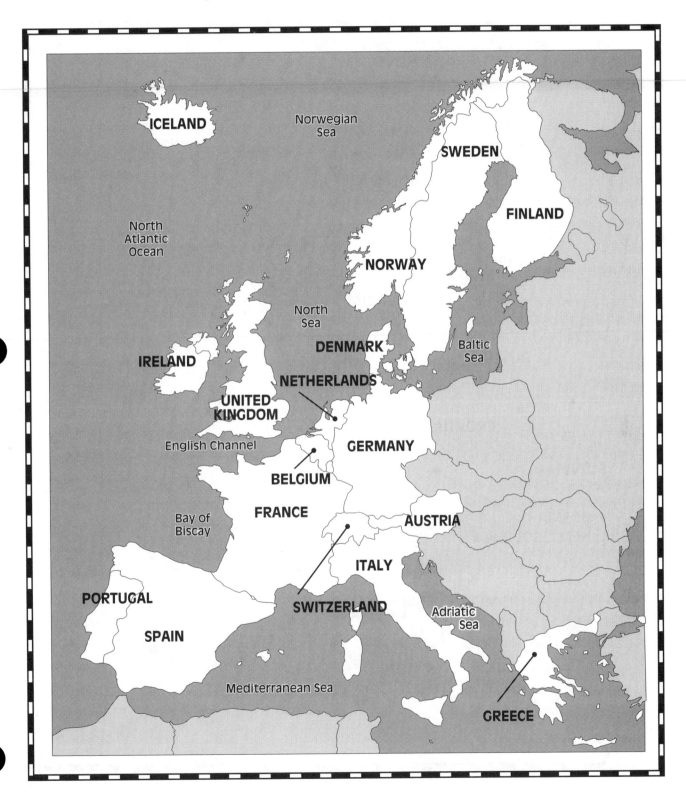

A Global Foods Tour Map Portfolio

Map 7
Eastern Europe

POLAND

Russia and
Neighboring Countries

CZECH
REPUBLIC

SLOVAKIA

AUSTRIA

HUNGARY

ROMANIA

CROATIA

SLOVENIA

Black
Sea

BOSNIA-
HERCEGOVINIA

SERBIA

BULGARIA

Adriatic
Sea

MACEDONIA

MONTENEGRO

ALBANIA

Aegean
Sea

A Global Foods Tour Map Portfolio

Map 8
Eastern Europe and Northern Asia

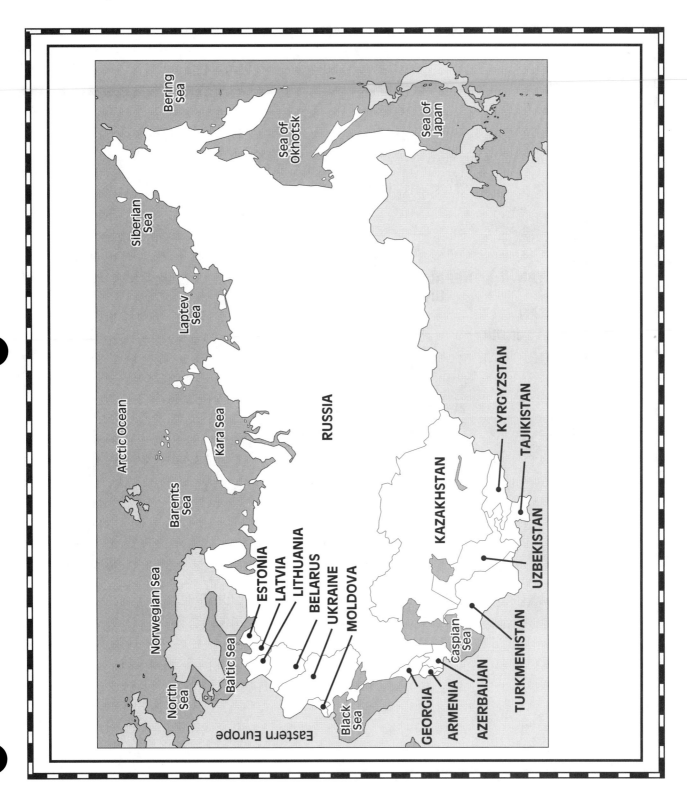

A Global Foods Tour Map Portfolio

Map 9
East and Southeast Asia

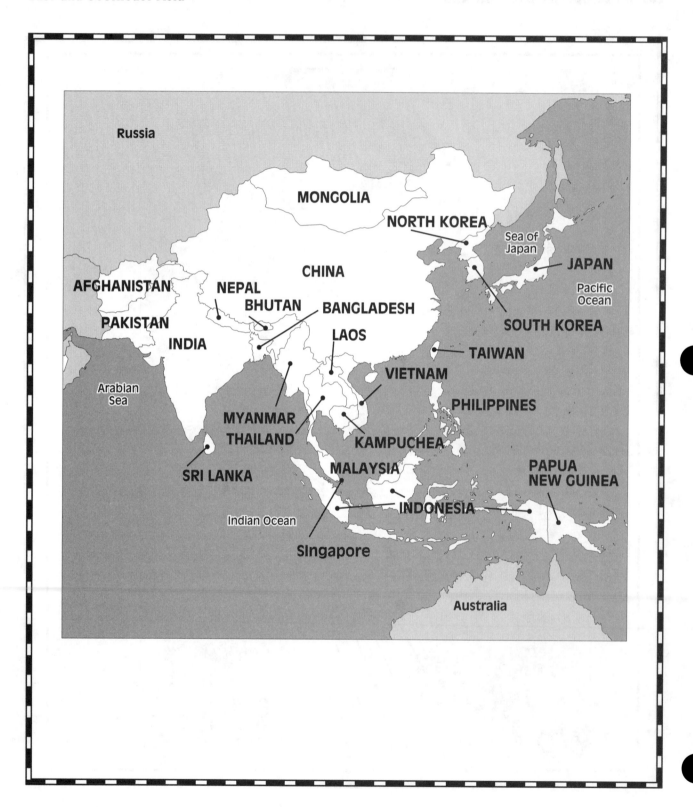

A Global Foods Tour Map Portfolio

Map 10

Southwest Asia and North Africa

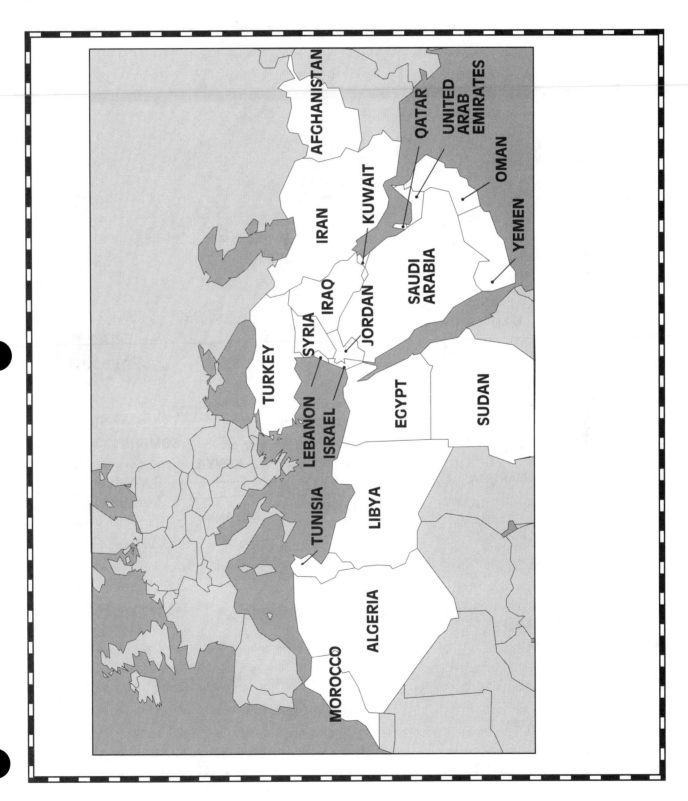

A Global Foods Tour Map Portfolio

Map 11
Africa

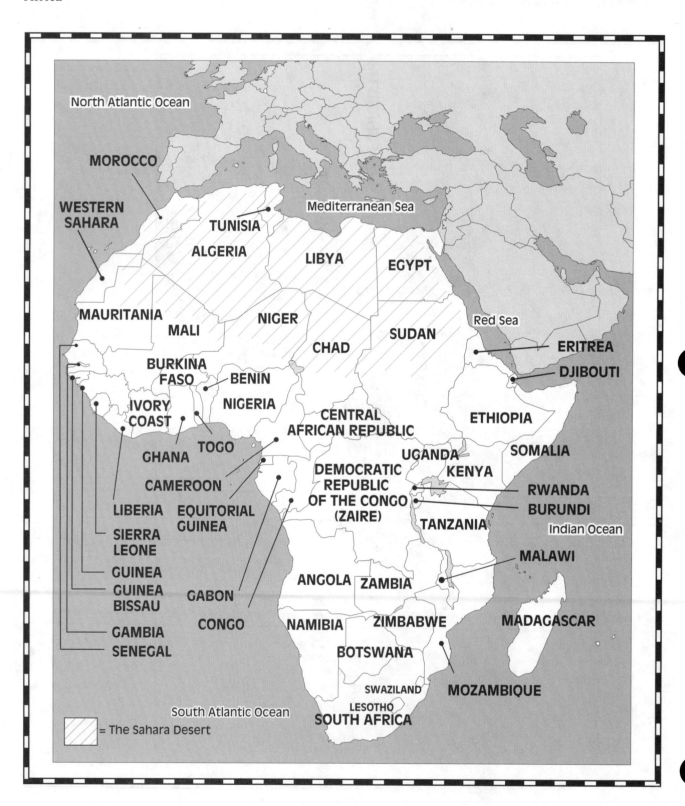

North Atlantic Ocean

MOROCCO

WESTERN SAHARA

Mediterranean Sea

TUNISIA

ALGERIA

LIBYA

EGYPT

MAURITANIA

MALI

NIGER

SUDAN

Red Sea

CHAD

ERITREA

BURKINA FASO

BENIN

DJIBOUTI

NIGERIA

IVORY COAST

CENTRAL AFRICAN REPUBLIC

ETHIOPIA

GHANA

TOGO

UGANDA

SOMALIA

CAMEROON

DEMOCRATIC REPUBLIC OF THE CONGO (ZAIRE)

KENYA

LIBERIA

EQUITORIAL GUINEA

RWANDA

BURUNDI

SIERRA LEONE

TANZANIA

Indian Ocean

GUINEA

MALAWI

GUINEA BISSAU

GABON

ANGOLA

ZAMBIA

GAMBIA

CONGO

ZIMBABWE

MADAGASCAR

SENEGAL

NAMIBIA

BOTSWANA

MOZAMBIQUE

SWAZILAND

South Atlantic Ocean

LESOTHO

SOUTH AFRICA

= The Sahara Desert

A Global Foods Tour Map Portfolio

Map 12
Australia and Oceania

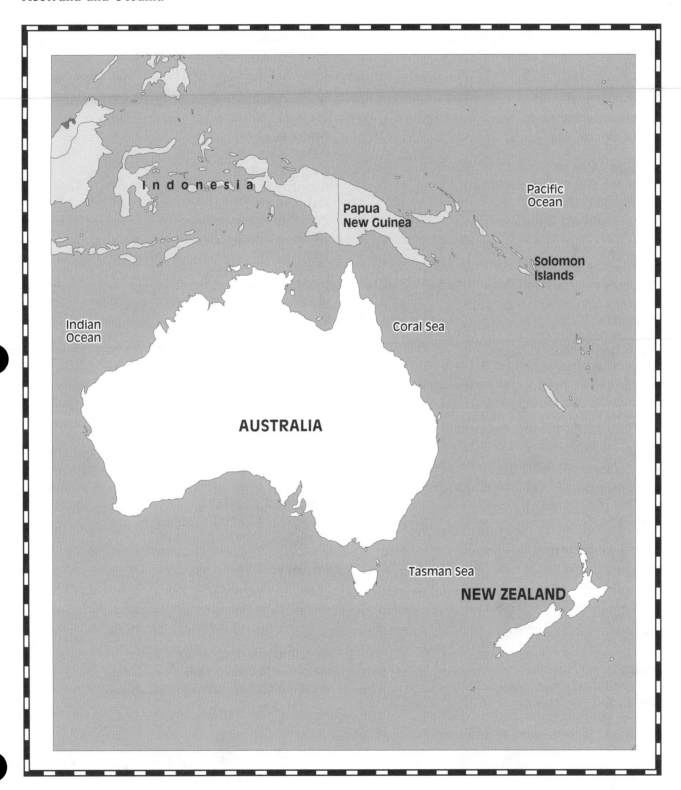

A Global Foods Tour Recipe Index

M = Includes microwave directions

Appetizers
Ceviche (Recipe 13) *M*
Cornish Pasties (Recipe 19)
Hummus bi Tahini (Recipe 41)
Knishes with Potato Filling (Recipe 37)
Maki-Sushi (Recipe 28)
Tortilla de Patatas (Recipe 16) *M*

Breads—Quick
Blintzes (Recipe 40)
Injera (Recipe 46)

Breads—Yeast
Russian Black Bread (Recipe 23)
Soft Pretzels (Recipe 2)
Sourdough Bread (Recipe 4)

Cheese
Blintzes (Recipe 40)
Chayotes Rellenos con Queso (Recipe 15) *M*

Desserts
Blintzes (Recipe 40)
Cherry-Plum Cobbler (Recipe 7)
Dobos Torta (Recipe 27)
Maple Walnut Tourlouche (Recipe 10)
Pavlova (Recipe 49)
Rollos de Coco (Recipe 11)

Eggs
Avgolemono (Recipe 25)
Egyptian Eggplant Omelet (Recipe 36)
Pavlova (Recipe 49)
Tortilla de Patatas (Recipe 16) *M*

Fish and Shellfish
Ceviche (Recipe 13) M
Fish Curry (Recipe 34)
Lomi Lomi Salmon (Recipe 6)
Perok (Recipe 5)
U'nega'gei (Recipe 9)

Fruits
Cherry-Plum cobbler (Recipe 7)
Mango and Coconut Chutney (Recipe 35)
Pavlova (Recipe 49)
Rollos de Coco (Recipe 11)

Grains (also see Rice)
Baked Kibbe (Recipe 38) *M*
Kasha (Recipe 24)
Polenta con Salsa di Pomodoro (Recipe 18)
Tamales (Recipe 12)

Legumes
Boston Baked Beans (Recipe 1)
Dal (Recipe 32)
Hummus bi Tahini (Recipe 41)
Peanut Soup (Recipe 42) *M*

Main Dishes
Baked Kibbe (Recipe 38) *M*
Chili (Recipe 8)
Curried Meat Patties (Recipe 33)
Dal (Recipe 32)
Fish Curry (Recipe 34)
Goulash (Recipe 26)
Lamb Chops with Orange Sauce (47)
Mole Poblano (Recipe 14)
Perok (Recipe 5)
Steamed Ginger Chicken (Recipe 29)
Tamales (Recipe 12)

Meats
Baked Kibbe (Recipe 38) *M*
Cornish Pasties (Recipe 19)
Chili (Recipe 8)
Curried Meat Patties (Recipe 33)
Goulash (Recipe 26)
Lamb Chops with Orange Sauce (Recipe 47)
Smorrebrod with Frikadeller (Recipe 21)

Nuts and Seeds
Hummus bi Tahini (Recipe 41)
Peanut Soup (Recipe 42) *M*

Poultry
Mole Poblano (Recipe 14)
Steamed Ginger Chicken (Recipe 29)

Rice
Avgolemono (Recipe 25)
Maki-Sushi (Recipe 28)
West African Yellow Rice (Recipe 45)

(Continued on next page)

Salads and Dressings

Chicken Salad with Fruit and Rice (Recipe 48)
Chinese Bean Sprout Salad (Recipe 30)
Eggplant Salad with Yogurt Dressing (Recipe 39) *M*
Lomi Lomi Salmon (Recipe 6)

Sandwiches

Smorrebrod with Frikadeller (Recipe 21)

Snacks

Hummus bi Tahini (Recipe 41)
Knishes with Potato Filling (Recipe 37)
Soft Pretzels (Recipe 2)

Sauces

Polenta con Salsa di Pomodoro (Recipe 22)
Mango and Coconut Chutney (Recipe 35)

Soups

Avgolemono (Recipe 25)
Borscht (Recipe 22)
Peanut Soup (Recipe 42) *M*
U'nega'gei (Recipe 9)

Vegetables

Blaukraut (Recipe 20) *M*
Borscht (Recipe 22)
Chayotes Rellenos con Queso (Recipe 15) *M*
Chinese Bean Sprout Salad (Recipe 30)
Eggplant Salad with Yogurt Dressing (Recipe 39) *M*
Fufu (Recipe 44) *M*
Kenya Greens with Lemon (Recipe 43)
Kimchi (Recipe 31)

Knishes with Potato Filling (Recipe 37)
Ratatouille (Recipe 17)
Sautéed Greens (Recipe 3)
Tortilla de Patatas (Recipe 16) *M*

Yogurt

Eggplant Salad with Yogurt Dressing (Recipe 39) *M*

NOTES

◆ Microwave Preparation. Results will vary depending on the characteristics of individual microwave ovens. Microwave recipes should be tested using your equipment before allowing students to prepare them. It may be necessary to modify the directions in order to achieve best results with the oven(s) used. Consult the microwave oven owner's manual or cooking guide for further suggestions.

◆ Nutrition Information. Selected information on nutrient content is provided following each recipe. All values given are approximate. The information is obtained from a computer analysis based on recipe ingredients and a database of nutrient values.

◆ Metric and Customary Equivalents. Because in many cases a precise numerical calculation would yield an impractical result, this book uses approximate equivalents that are easy to measure using standard metric and customary equipment. For example, instead of the precise equivalent of 1 cup = 236 mL, this book uses 1 cup = 250 mL.

A Global Foods Tour Recipe Worksheet

Name of Recipe: _____

Planning the Lab

1. List the equipment you need to prepare this recipe:

   _____

   _____

   _____

   _____

2. On a separate sheet of paper, make a work plan for preparing this recipe in the foods lab.

Questions

1. How does this recipe reflect the food traditions of its native country or region?

   _____

   _____

2. How would you rate the nutritional value of this recipe? Why?

   _____

   _____

Evaluation

After preparing the recipe, complete the following:

1. How did the food look and taste?

   _____

   _____

2. What changes would you want to make in the recipe? Why?

   _____

   _____

3. List any difficulties you had in preparing the recipe.

   _____

   _____

4. How would you solve the problem(s) next time?

   _____

   _____

Touring the U.S.A.

A Global Foods Tour

To say that the United States stretches "from sea to shining sea" is quite accurate. This third largest country in the world does indeed reach from the Atlantic Ocean to the Pacific Ocean. In between the two coasts are an incredible variety of landscapes. Consider the majestic snowcapped peaks of the Rocky Mountains, the orderly wheat fields of the Midwest, and the expanses of desert in Arizona and New Mexico. Add to these the bays and harbors of New England, the chilly blue lakes of Michigan and Minnesota, and the cotton fields of the South. Include the skyscrapers of New York City and the sunny beaches of the Gulf of Mexico, and you will have an idea of the geographical diversity that makes up the United States.

People and Cultures

Sometimes called a "melting pot," the United States is truly a unique blend of dozens of different cultures. Many Americans are descendants of European settlers who came to the United States in waves beginning in the 1500s. These Americans are descended from the British, German, French, Spanish, Italian, Scandinavian, and many other nationalities. African-Americans and Hispanics, who have both added their own rich traditions to the "melting pot," are the second-largest and third-largest groups. Asians and Pacific Islanders, followed by Native Americans, round out the population. Throughout the country, the languages, foods, and traditions of these cultures mingle to create a delicious mixture of diversity!

Cuisines of the United States

A food tour of the United States would include a very wide spectrum of meals! The variety of climates and landforms of this large country ensures that different foods are produced in the various regions. The seafood that is so common in menus of the coastal states is likely to be replaced by beef and pork as you travel further inland. While you might be served sweet potato pie in the Southeast (where most sweet potatoes are grown), you are more likely to be served a berry pie in the fruit-growing states of the Northwest. Not only are these regional cuisines affected by the locally grown foods, they are affected by the local people, as well! As various ethnic groups settled in certain parts of the United States, they influenced the foods of those areas. For example, because many people of Mexican descent live in the Southwestern states, foods in this region tend to resemble those of Mexico. Along the Pacific Coast, where there is a large Asian population, many dishes feature fish and rice. Whatever kind of food you like, you are almost sure to find it on a foods tour of the United States!

The Savvy Gourmet

At one time, regional foods of the United States were so distinct that they were associated with a single place and no other. Technology has caused many regional foods to lose their identities. Key lime pie is an example. At first made only in the Florida Keys, where the limes once grew, the makings now come in a box, and this treat is served and enjoyed all over the country.

Port of Call

Northeastern Region

Touring the U.S.A.

The Northeastern Region of the United States starts with the far-north state of Maine and extends southward to include the other New England States of New Hampshire, Vermont, Massachusetts, Rhode Island, and Connecticut. Also included in this region are the coastal states of New Jersey and Delaware, which lie south of the New England States. The states of New York and Pennsylvania, which are tucked in behind the smaller coastal states, complete the Northeastern Region.

Food Traveler's Notes

Climate and Agriculture

Hay and the dairy cattle that eat it thrive in the cool, damp climate of the Northeast. Maine, New York, Pennsylvania, and Vermont are important dairy states, producing great quantities of milk, cheese, and butter. The food most often associated with the Northeastern Region, however, is the wide array of seafood caught off the Atlantic Coast. Another food commonly associated with this region is fruit. Certain Northeastern states are famous for specific fruits. You may see advertisements for "Maine blueberries" or "Massachusetts cranberries," for example.

People and Language

The Northeastern States were first settled by the English, and many of the people living there today are descendants of those early settlers. This region has also been the first stopping-off point for wave after wave of immigrants. As a result, the people of the Northeastern Region represent a rich variety of ancestries and cultures. In the larger cities of the Northeast—such as New York City, Boston, and Philadelphia—you can find people, foods, and languages from around the world. Throughout the region are large populations of the first settlers—Germans, Italians, Irish, and French Canadians—all with their own traditions and food preferences.

Food and Cuisine

Seafood is a "must" on a food tour of the Northeastern Region. Here, the chilly gray waters of the Atlantic Ocean produce some of the most famous seafood in the world. You won't meet many people who haven't heard of New England clam chowder. Maine lobster is equally well known. People of the Northeastern Region eat seafood in any number of ways: baked, broiled, grilled, fried, poached, or made into stews, soups, casseroles, and salads.

Some of the most popular dishes of the Northeastern Region reflect the tastes of its earliest settlers. For example, the New England boiled dinner—a corned beef brisket boiled in water with cabbage, potatoes, and other vegetables—has its roots in English cuisine. The Native Americans influenced early Northeastern cuisine by introducing new ingredients like corn and beans. To see how these ingredients are still used today, you might stop by Massachusetts to sample its famous Boston baked beans or some cornmeal-based Boston brown bread.

Looking Back on the Northeastern Region

1. Chowder is a favorite dish in the Northeastern Region. Research chowder to find out what it consists of. How does it differ from soup? There are two different types of clam chowder. How do they differ? Write a report on your findings.

2. Which other foods do you associate with the Northeastern Region? Why? List the states in this region and next to each one, write down the foods you associate with it.

Southern Region

From the long, skinny arm of Florida, the Southern Region of the United States sprawls northward and westward through the hot cotton-growing states of Georgia, Alabama, Mississippi, and Louisiana. Spreading further north, the region includes the inland states of Arkansas, Tennessee, Kentucky, and West Virginia. Also in this region are the warm, humid states along the southern half of the East Coast: South Carolina, North Carolina, Virginia, and Maryland.

Food Traveler's Notes

Climate and Agriculture

The long, warm summers, mild winters, and plentiful rainfall make this part of the United States ideal for growing certain kinds of crops. Although cotton is a leading crop of the region, farmers here also grow peanuts, soybeans, corn, sweet potatoes, rice, and, of course, fruit! From this region come the famous Florida citrus fruits and Georgia peaches. Poultry farming is also important. The Southern states raise more broiler chickens than any other region of the United States, so visitors here should be sure to sample the delicious Southern-fried chicken!

People and Language

The many Native Americans who originally lived in the Southern Region were joined in the 17th and 18th centuries by European settlers, mostly from Spain, France, and Britain. Today, many people living in the Southern Region are descendants of these Native Americans and European settlers. Another large part of the population in this region is made up of African Americans. Many of these African Americans are descended from African peoples who were brought to America as slaves in the 18th century. The population of Florida also includes a large number of Latin Americans.

Food and Cuisine

The foods of the Southern Region are a delicious mixture of Native American, African, and European flavors and textures. Corn was one of the first foods the Native Americans introduced to the Southern settlers. For decades, people of this region have simmered dried corn kernels, called hominy, with milk or water to make a dish called grits. Cornbread and hush puppies are two other Southern favorites made with corn. When the Africans came to America, they brought with them their own tastes and food preparation methods. They developed new recipes such as collard greens cooked with salt pork and chitterlings—bits of fried hog intestine. European influences on foods can be seen throughout the region, but especially in the Cajun and Creole cuisines of Louisiana. Both of these cuisines are an interesting blend of French and American traditions. Cajun and Creole specialties include a number of thick stews and soups, called gumbos, jambalayas, or bisques.

Looking Back on the Southern Region

1. Citrus fruits and peaches are two of the Southern Region's most common fruits. Why do you think these fruits might be common here but not in other regions? Share your thoughts with the class in a discussion.

2. Which other foods do you associate with the Southern Region? Why? Find recipes that feature those foods. Share your research with the class.

Port of Call

Pacific Coast Region

Touring the U.S.A.

The states of Washington, Oregon, and California make up the Pacific Coast Region of the United States. They stretch from the very top of the United States, where Washington meets British Columbia, to the very bottom, where California meets Mexico. Although it lies about 2,400 miles (3860 km) southwest of the U.S. mainland, Hawaii may be grouped with these states. On the island of Hawaii is Ka Lea—which means South Point—the farthest point south in the United States. If you travel north from Hawaii, you will eventually run into Alaska, the largest state of the United States and the most northern point of the United States.

Food Traveler's Notes

Climate and Agriculture

Between the rugged mountains that are part of the Pacific Coast Region lie some of the nation's most fertile valleys. This area produces a large part of the nation's fruits, nuts, and vegetables. Washington produces more apples than any other state, while California leads the nation in most other fruits and vegetables. The fertile fields of California are home to almost every kind of crop that is grown anywhere in the United States.

The direct access of these states to the Pacific Ocean has also led to the development of a large fishing and seafood industry. All along the Pacific Coast, fishing ships bring in a wide array of treasures for the seafood lover—clams, crabs, oysters, shrimp, salmon, and other kinds of fish.

People and Language

Today the Pacific Coast is home to African Americans and Mexican Americans as well as people of European ancestry. This region also has more people of Asian ancestry than any other region of the United States. In addition, a large number of Native Americans live here. On the streets of San Francisco, Seattle, or any other large Pacific Coast city, you may hear English, Spanish, or any number of Asian languages spoken.

Food and Cuisine

The cuisine of the Pacific Coast Region is known for its freshness and flavor. Fresh ingredients are the key. The California style of food preparation relies on simplicity and lively tastes. California cooks use tangy marinades, vinaigrettes, and salsas to create interesting and unique flavor combinations in their dishes. Meats and vegetables are often grilled or roasted quickly in a high-temperature oven. Today, many restaurants throughout the country offer "California Cuisine."

Foods of the Pacific Coast have been influenced by the region's neighbors—Mexico to the south and the Asian countries across the ocean. As you travel through Southern California, you might expect to find the chili-spiced dishes of Mexico. Further up the coast, where there are large Asian populations, you may find dishes that feature fresh seafood and rice. In Hawaii, you will also find seafood dishes—but with a tropical twist! Hawaiian dishes often include the delicious flavors of pineapple, coconut, and mango.

Looking Back on the Pacific Coast Region

1. Lobsters are found in both the Atlantic and Pacific oceans. Research lobsters to find out how they differ. Write a paragraph summarizing what you discover.

2. Which foods do you most associate with the Pacific Coast Region? Why? Which of these foods have you tried? Share your answers with the class. As a class, prepare posters featuring those foods.

Port of Call
Midwestern Region

Touring the U.S.A.

Sometimes called the "Heartland," the Midwestern Region is a mostly flat, fertile expanse of land nestled in between the Rocky Mountains on the West and the Appalachian Mountains on the East. The region's most eastern point is the state of Ohio, and its western edge is made up of North Dakota, South Dakota, Nebraska, Kansas, and Oklahoma. Between these two boundaries lie the states of Michigan, Indiana, Illinois, Wisconsin, Minnesota, Iowa, and Missouri.

Food Traveler's Notes

Climate and Agriculture

If you look down at the Midwestern states from an airplane, you will see square blocks of fields that stretch for miles. This region of the country—with cold winters, warm summers, good soil, and plenty of rainfall—is largely farmland. Most of the nation's corn, soybeans, and wheat come from these states. The corn that is raised throughout the Midwest makes excellent feed for the region's large population of livestock. Cattle and hogs thrive here, and many of the Midwestern states are among the top producers in the United States of both beef cattle and hogs. Dairy products are also important in this region, especially in the states of Minnesota and Wisconsin; Wisconsin is even nicknamed "the Dairy State."

People and Language

The states of the Midwest were settled by pioneers from the East. The largest groups were the Germans, Swedes, Norwegians, and Irish. Many of the people living in these states today are descended from Europeans. There are also populations of Native Americans, African-Americans, and Asians.

Food and Cuisine

The cuisine of the Midwestern Region tends to be hearty and simple, developed to nourish the hardworking farmers who settled the land. Many meals feature prime cuts of meat from the corn-fed cattle and hogs of the region. Roasts, pork chops, spareribs, steaks, ham, and meat loaves are all common main dishes here. To sample some of the best Midwestern beef, you might stop in Omaha, Nebraska, for a thick, juicy steak or in Kansas City, Missouri, for some delicious barbecue. In Cincinnati, Ohio, you can taste some of the city's famous chili. When eating a meal in the Midwest, you will almost certainly be served some of the area's vegetables—perhaps green beans, corn on the cob, mashed potatoes, or stewed tomatoes—as a side dish. Don't forget the bread! Midwesterners use their staple crops of corn and wheat to make a wide variety of breads.

Looking Back on the Midwestern Region

1. Freshwater fish, such as perch, walleye, pike, and catfish, are more common than seafood in traditional Midwestern cuisine. Why do you suppose this is the case? Explain your reasoning in a short report.

2. Which foods do you most associate with the Midwestern Region? Why? Plan a menu using foods from this region. Share your menu plan with the class.

Port of Call
Northwestern and Southwestern Region

Touring the U.S.A.

Covering a broad sweep of land from the Canadian border to the Mexican border are the states of the Northwestern and Southwestern Region. The defining feature of most of this region is the Rocky Mountain range, which sweeps through the western part of Montana southward through Idaho, Wyoming, Utah, Colorado, and New Mexico. The region also includes the desert states of Nevada and Arizona, as well as Texas, the only state of the region with a coastline.

Food Traveler's Notes

Climate and Agriculture

Much of the dry, mountainous land of the Northwestern and Southwestern Region is not well-suited to crop farming. Therefore livestock ranching is much more important than farming. Practically all of the states in this region raise large numbers of beef cattle and sheep. Texas is perhaps the most productive agricultural state of the area, producing cattle, sheep, rice, wheat, citrus fruits, and vegetables. Another important agricultural state is Idaho, home of the well-known Idaho potato!

People and Language

The Southwestern states, because of their nearness to Mexico, are home to a large number of Hispanic people. In both Texas and New Mexico more than 25 percent of the population is made up of Hispanics, many of whom speak both English and Spanish. A large number of Native Americans also live in this region, especially in New Mexico. The states further north contain a mixture of cultures: Native Americans, Hispanics, and descendants of European settlers. Colorado, especially, has a diverse blend of cultures. This stems partly from the days of the Gold Rush, when groups of people from all over Europe and North America settled in Colorado in hopes of finding their fortunes.

Food and Cuisine

There is much difference between the foods in the Northwestern and Southwestern region. If you travel through the Southwestern states of Texas, New Mexico, and Arizona, you will find a cuisine that resembles that of Mexico. Such chili-spiced dishes as tamales, tacos, and chili con carne are common here. In Texas, this south-of-the-border cuisine has been modified somewhat to include elements of both Texas and Mexico. Called Tex-Mex, this style of food preparation tends to use more meats and cheeses than traditional Mexican cuisine.

As you travel further north, you will find more European influences on foods. For example, two popular foods in Utah are a spiced red cabbage dish and a lima bean-and-sausage casserole, both of which come from German cuisine. In the most northern states in this region, freshwater fish and game animals play an important role in many meals. When dining here, you may be served pan-fried trout, smoked wild turkey, or roast venison!

Looking Back on the Northwestern and Southwestern Region

1. Chilies are an important part of many dishes in the Southwestern states but not in the Northwestern states. Prepare a short report explaining why this might be the case.

2. Which do you think you would prefer: the foods of the Northwest or of the Southwest? Share your thoughts in a class discussion.

Boston Baked Beans

Recipe 1

Touring Northeastern Region U.S.A.

Boston Baked Beans

Customary	Ingredients	Metric
4 cups	Water	1 L
1¹/₄ cups	Dry navy beans, sorted and rinsed	300 mL
	Water	
¹/₄ cup	Onion, chopped	50 mL
2 Tbsp.	Dark molasses	30 mL
2 Tbsp.	Brown sugar	30 mL
1 tsp.	Dry mustard	5 mL
¹/₂ tsp.	Salt	2 mL
¹/₂ tsp.	Vinegar	2 mL
4 oz.	Salt pork	125 g

Yield: 4 servings

Directions

Pans: 2-quart (2-L) saucepan; 2-quart (2-L) casserole

1. Combine 4 cups (1 L) water and beans. Let soak overnight.

2. Drain and discard soaking water.

3. Add enough fresh water to cover beans. Bring to a boil. Reduce heat and simmer, covered, for 30 minutes.

4. Drain beans and reserve cooking water.

5. In casserole, combine beans, ¹/₂ cup (125 mL) reserved cooking water, chopped onion, molasses, brown sugar, dry mustard, salt, and vinegar.

6. Cut salt pork into 4 pieces. Press into surface of beans.

7. Cover casserole. Bake at 250°F (120°C) for 6 to 8 hours. If beans begin to dry out during cooking, add more reserved cooking water, heated to boiling; do not stir. (Beans should be moist but not soupy.) During last 30 to 60 minutes of cooking, uncover beans to let them brown.

8. Discard salt pork before serving.

Nutrition Information: Serving size: ³/₄ cup (175 mL)

calories: 126
total fat: 1 g
saturated fat: 0 g
cholesterol: 0 mg
sodium: 289 mg

carbohydrate: 26 g
dietary fiber: 3 g
sugars: 11 g
protein: 5 g

Percent Daily Value: vitamin A 6%, vitamin C 1%, calcium 14%, iron 23%

Soft Pretzels

(Pennsylvania Dutch)

Soft Pretzels
(Pennsylvania Dutch)

Customary	Ingredients	Metric
1/4 oz. pkg.	Active dry yeast	7 g pkg.
1/4 cup	Brown sugar	50 mL
1 1/2 cups	Warm water, about 85°F (30°C)	350 mL
5 cups	All-purpose flour	1.25 L
4 cups	Water	1 L
1 1/2 Tbsp.	Baking soda	22 mL
	Coarse or kosher salt (optional)	

Yield: About 12 large pretzels

Directions

Pans: Large saucepan or Dutch oven; baking sheets

1. Preheat oven to 475°F (240°C). Grease baking sheets.

2. Combine yeast and brown sugar in large bowl. Gradually add 1 1/2 cups (350 mL) warm water, stirring until yeast is dissolved. Let stand 5 minutes.

3. Stir in flour; blend well.

4. Turn dough out onto lightly floured surface. Knead until smooth and elastic, 5 to 10 minutes.

5. Pinch or slice off enough dough to form a 1 1/2-inch (4-cm) ball. On lightly floured surface, roll ball into a rope and shape into a pretzel.

6. Combine 4 cups (1 L) water and baking soda in saucepan; bring to a boil.

7. Lift pretzels with spatula and drop into boiling water, a few at a time. Boil until pretzels rise to the surface, about 1 minute.

8. Place pretzels on greased baking sheets. Sprinkle with salt, if desired.

9. Bake at 475°F (240°C) for 8 minutes. Serve warm.

Nutrition Information: Serving size: 1 pretzel

calories: 193
total fat: 0 g
saturated fat: 0 g
cholesterol: 0 mg
sodium: 210 mg

carbohydrate: 41 g
dietary fiber: 1 g
sugars: 5 g
protein: 5 g

Percent Daily Value: vitamin A 0%, vitamin C 0%, calcium 1%, iron 16%

Sautéed Greens

Sautéed Greens

Customary	Ingredients	Metric
1¹/₂ lb.	Cooking greens (beet greens, collards, kale, mustard greens, Swiss chard, or turnip greens)	750 g
¹/₂ cup	Diced lean ham	125 mL
¹/₄ cup	Chopped onion	50 mL
2 tsp.	Vinegar	10 mL
¹/₈ tsp.	Pepper	0.5 mL

Yield: 4 servings

Directions

Pan: Skillet

1. Wash and drain greens. Trim off tough stems. Chop or tear large leaves into pieces.

2. Sauté ham in skillet until browned. Remove ham and set aside.

3. Sauté onion in ham drippings until soft.

4. Add greens, vinegar, and pepper. Cover. Cook over medium heat, stirring occasionally, until greens are tender, about 10 to 15 minutes.

5. Return ham to skillet. Mix well and heat through. Serve hot.

Nutrition Information: Serving size: ¹/₄ recipe

calories: 76
total fat: 1 g
saturated fat: 0 g
cholesterol: 9 mg
sodium: 620 mg

carbohydrate: 11 g
dietary fiber: 5 g
sugars: 0.4 g
protein: 8 g

Percent Daily Value: vitamin A 108%, vitamin C 77%, calcium 24%, iron 23%

Tips for Success

◆ The flavor of greens varies from the mild, cabbage-like flavor of kale to the sharp taste of mustard greens.
◆ Wash greens in several changes of cool water. Drain well or blot dry.

Sourdough Bread

Sourdough Starter

Recipe 4

Touring Pacific Coast Region U.S.A.

Sourdough Starter (Yield: About 3 cups (750 mL))

Customary	Ingredients	Metric
2 cups	All-purpose flour	500 mL
1/4-oz. pkg.	Active dry yeast	7-g pkg.
1/2 tsp.	Sugar	2 mL
2 cups	Warm water, about 85°F (30°C)	500 mL

Directions

1. Stir together flour, yeast, and sugar. Gradually stir in water. Beat until smooth.
2. Cover tightly; set in a warm place, about 85°F (30°C), for 2 to 3 days. Stir down once or twice a day.
3. Starter is ready to use when it is frothy and has a sour, yeasty odor. Stir well before using. Refrigerate left-over starter.

Sourdough Bread

Customary	Ingredients	Metric
1 cup	Sourdough starter (above)	250 mL
1 1/2 cups	Warm water, about 85°F (30°C)	350 mL
2 Tbsp.	Margarine, softened	30 mL
1 Tbsp.	Honey or molasses	15 mL
1 tsp.	Salt	5 mL
6 cups	All-purpose flour (divided)	1.5 L
1/2 tsp.	Baking soda	2 mL
	Vegetable oil	

Yield: 2 loaves

Directions

Pans: Two 9 x 5 x 3 inch (23 x 13 x 8 cm) loaf pans

1. In large bowl, mix starter, water, margarine, honey or molasses, and salt.
2. Gradually add 4 cups (1L) flour and baking soda. Mix thoroughly.
3. Let mixture stand uncovered in a warm place, about 85°F (30°C), overnight.
4. Stir in 1 cup (250 mL) flour until well combined.
5. Turn dough out onto bread board covered with remaining 1 cup (250 mL) flour. Knead until dough is smooth and elastic.
6. Divide dough into two portions. Shape each into a loaf. Place in greased loaf pans.
7. Brush top of loaves with vegetable oil. Cover with plastic wrap and clean dish towel. Let rise in a warm place until doubled in size, about 2 hours.
8. Bake at 400°F (200°C) for 45 to 50 minutes or until loaves sound hollow when tapped.
9. Remove loaves from pans and cool on rack.

Nutrition Information: Serving size: One 3/4-inch (2 cm) slice (1/24 recipe)

calories: 128	cholesterol: 0 mg	dietary fiber: 1 g
total fat: 1 g	sodium: 118 mg	sugars: 1 g
saturated fat: 0 g	carbohydrate: 25 g	protein: 3 g

Percent Daily Value: vitamin A 1%, vitamin C 3%, calcium 0%, iron 10%

Perok
(Fish Pie)

Perok
(Fish Pie)

Customary	Ingredients	Metric
	Pastry	
2 cups	All-purpose flour	500 mL
1/2 cup	Vegetable oil	125 mL
3 Tbsp.	Cold water	45 mL
	Filling	
1/2 lb.	Halibut	250 g
2 cups	Rice, cooked	500 mL
1/2 cup	Onions, chopped	125 mL
2	Hard-cooked eggs, chopped	2
1/2 tsp.	Salt	2 mL
1/2 tsp.	Pepper	2 mL

Yield: 8 servings

Directions

Pan: 9-inch (23 cm) pie pan

1. Cut halibut into 1-inch (2.5 cm) thick pieces.
2. Preheat oven to 350°F (180°C).
3. Add oil to flour, mixing well with fork. Sprinkle 3 Tbsp. (45 mL) cold water over pastry mixture, mixing well with fork.
4. Divide pastry in half and form into two balls. Place each pastry ball between two sheets of waxed paper. Roll out to 11-inch (28 cm) circles.
5. Peel off top sheet of waxed paper from one pastry circle. Invert pastry into 9-inch (23 cm) pie pan. Peel off second sheet of waxed paper. Fit pastry carefully into pie pan. Trim overhanging pastry 1/2 (1.25 cm) inch from edge of pan.
6. Spread 1 cup (250 mL) cooked rice over pastry-lined pan. Place the halibut on top of the rice. Spread the chopped onion and hard-cooked eggs over the halibut. Add salt and pepper. Spread the remaining 1 cup (250 mL) of rice over the halibut, onions, and eggs.
7. Peel off top sheet of waxed paper from remaining 11-inch (28 cm) pastry circle; make several slits for steam vents. Invert pastry over filling. Peel off second sheet of waxed paper.
8. Trim top crust 1 inch (2.5 cm) beyond edge of pie pan. Fold top crust under bottom crust and crimp edge.
9. Bake 30 to 35 minutes or until crust is golden brown.

Variation: 1/2 lb. (250 g) fresh or 8 oz. canned (250 g) salmon can be substituted for halibut.

Nutrition information: Serving size: 1/8 of pie (using halibut)

calories: 329	cholesterol: 62 mg	dietary fiber: 1 g
total fat: 16 g	sodium 166 mg	sugars: 0.8 g
saturated fat: 2 g	carbohydrate 34 g	protein 12 g

Lomi Lomi Salmon

Lomi Lomi Salmon

Customary	Ingredients	Metric
15-oz. can	Drained salmon	470-g can
1 cup	Chopped tomato	250 mL
1 cup	Sliced onion	250 mL
2 tsp.	Lemon juice	10 mL
$1/2$ tsp.	Tarragon	2 mL
$1/4$ tsp.	Pepper	1 mL
8 leaves	Romaine lettuce	8 leaves

Yield: 8 servings

Directions

1. Combine salmon, tomato, and onion.

2. Sprinkle with lemon juice, tarragon, and pepper. Toss gently.

3. Cover and refrigerate at least 1 hour.

4. To serve, place one lettuce leaf on each of 8 salad plates. Top with $1/3$ to $1/2$ cup (75 mL to 125 mL) of salmon mixture.

Nutrition Information: Serving size: $1/8$ recipe

calories: 90
total fat: 3 g
saturated fat: 1 g
cholesterol: 29 mg
sodium: 345 mg

carbohydrate: 4 g
dietary fiber: 1 g
sugars: 1 g
protein: 11 g

Percent Daily Value: vitamin A 8%, vitamin C 16%, calcium 16%, iron 5%

Cherry-Plum Cobbler

Recipe 7

Touring Midwestern Region U.S.A.

Cherry-Plum Cobbler

Customary	Ingredients	Metric
3 cups	Cherries, pitted	750 mL
2 cups	Red plum slices	500 mL
1 cup	Sugar	250 mL
3 Tbsp.	Cornstarch	45 mL
1/2 tsp.	Cinnamon	2 mL
1 cup	All-purpose flour	250 mL
2 Tbsp.	Sugar	30 mL
1 1/2 tsp.	Baking powder	7 mL
1/2 tsp.	Salt	2 mL
1/4 cup	Shortening	50 mL
1/2 cup	Skim milk	125 mL

Yield: 8 servings

Directions

Pans: 2-qt. (2-L) heavy saucepan; 1 1/2-qt. (1.5-L) baking dish

1. Preheat oven to 375°F (190°C).

2. Combine cherries, plums, 1 cup (250 mL) sugar, cornstarch, and cinnamon in saucepan. Stir until well blended.

3. Cook over medium-low heat, stirring constantly, until mixture thickens and boils. Boil and stir for 1 minute.

4. Pour fruit mixture into baking dish.

5. Combine flour, 2 Tbsp. (30 mL) sugar, baking powder, and salt.

6. Cut shortening into dry ingredients until mixture resembles coarse crumbs.

7. Make a well in the center of the dry ingredients. Add milk. Stir to form a drop batter.

8. Drop batter in 8 spoonfuls on top of hot fruit mixture.

9. Bake at 375°F (190°C) until biscuit topping is golden brown, 25 to 30 minutes.

Nutrition Information: Serving size: 1/8 recipe

calories: 282
total fat: 7 g
saturated fat: 2 g
cholesterol: 0 mg
sodium: 138 mg

carbohydrate: 56 g
dietary fiber: 1 g
sugars: 34 g
protein: 3 g

Percent Daily Value: vitamin A 9%, vitamin C 5%, calcium 5%, iron 7%

Chili

Chili

Customary	Ingredients	Metric
3 lbs.	Ground beef	1.5 kg
1 medium	Chopped onion	1 medium
3 small cloves	Finely chopped garlic	3 small cloves
15-oz can	Tomato sauce	470-g can
5$1/2$ cups	Water	1.25 L
6 Tbsp. or to taste	Chili powder	90 mL or to taste
1 Tbsp.	Paprika	15 mL
1 Tbsp.	Crushed cumin seeds	15 mL
1 tsp.	Salt	5 mL
$1/2$ tsp.	Ground black pepper	2 mL

Yield: 8 to 10 servings

Directions

Pan: 2-qt. (2-L) saucepan

1. Combine ground beef, onion, and garlic in saucepan. Brown over medium heat, stirring to crumble.

2. Drain off pan drippings.

3. Add remaining ingredients. Mix well.

4. Cook over low heat for 3$1/2$ to 4 hours, stirring occasionally.

Nutrition Information: $1/10$ recipe

calories: 403
total fat: 22 g
saturated fat: 8 g
cholesterol: 134 mg
sodium: 390 mg

carbohydrate: 8 g
dietary fiber: 3 g
sugars: 0.4 g
protein: 41 g

Percent Daily Value: vitamin A 29%, vitamin C 12%, calcium 4%, iron 22%

Touring Canada

If you trace the southern border of Canada on Map 3 (page 18), you will see that a small part of Canada lies further south than some of the United States. Still, Canada is definitely North Country! Stretching north into the frigid regions of the Arctic Circle, Canada is the second-largest country in the world. If you travel from the east coast to the west coast of this country, you will pass through six time zones! Although Canada is large, much of it is too cold and harsh to support a large population. In spite of its great size, Canada's population is less than one-tenth of the United States' population. Three-quarters of all Canadians live in the southern portion of the country. The less-populated, northern regions are rugged wildernesses of frozen ground, inhabited by few people and a great variety of wildlife.

People and Cultures

Canada is divided into provinces and territories, which are similar to states in the United States. Each province or territory has its own character. The provinces of Ontario and Quebec contain more than half of Canada's population and its two largest cities—Montreal and Toronto. Research their locations and mark them on Map 3.

About 28 percent of the people in Canada are descended from the British. Another 25 percent are French Canadians. French Canadians keep the French culture alive in Canada by observing the language, traditions, and holidays of France. In the province of Quebec, where most French Canadians live, French is the primary language. Canadians in other provinces are descended from the Italian, German, Polish, Asian, and other peoples. Native Canadians, called "First Nations," make up most of the population of northern Canada.

Cuisines of Canada

Canadian cuisine reflects the many different lifestyles and ethnic groups that are found in Canada. Along the eastern and western coasts, you are likely to find fish and seafood on the menu. Apples, grapes, and blueberries are also common in these areas. In the rugged northern parts of the country, venison or moose might be a typical main course. Food in Quebec tends to have a French flavor, with thick soups and minced-meat pies being specialties. Canada is also famous for its maple syrup, which is often used in desserts.

The Savvy Gourmet

Most Canadians eat their main meal in the evening, usually between 6:00 and 7:30 P.M. Natives of Quebec consider this a family time, although guests are often invited. If you are scheduling a call, remember that many Canadians consider it rude to take or place a telephone call during this time.

Port of Call

Quebec

At three times the size of France, Quebec is Canada's largest province. It sits at the eastern end of Canada, bordered on the south by the United States' New England area. If you visit Quebec, you will notice that almost two-thirds of this large province is covered with forest. All throughout central and northern Quebec, you will travel through hills carpeted with evergreen trees and dotted with thousands of lakes. You might also see some of Quebec's many kinds of wildlife—perhaps a black bear, a caribou, or a moose! Toward the southern end of the province, the evergreen forest gives way to the Saint Lawrence Lowlands—a plain made up of the land bordering the Saint Lawrence River. This region is the heart of Quebec's agriculture, industry, and population. While in this area, you might stop for dinner in Montreal or Quebec City, two of the province's largest cities. If it is a seascape you prefer, you could travel along the coasts of Quebec. In the cold waters off these coasts, you might spot whales and seals, as well as a variety of saltwater fish. After whale watching, take a break and dine on some of Quebec's delicious fresh seafood!

Food Traveler's Notes

Agriculture

Milk is one of the most common agricultural products of Quebec. Almost half of the farms in this province specialize in dairy products. Pork, potatoes, and fruits are also common products of Quebec. Corn, hay, and oats are the major field crops. In addition, Quebec is famous for its maple syrup—a sweet, flavorful syrup made by boiling the sap of maple trees.

People and Language

More than seven million Canadians live in Quebec. More than 70 percent of that seven million are French Canadians. Most French Canadians are very proud of their heritage. They value the traditions of their culture including its language. Even though both French and English are official languages of Canada, you will hear mostly French spoken when you visit Quebec. The provincial government of Quebec encourages people to speak French instead of English.

Yet the culture of Quebec is not precisely French. It is, rather, a unique mixture of French and North American. Visitors may find that many Quebec inhabitants speak fluent English as a second language. In the larger cities like Toronto, people sometimes mix English and French in the same sentence!

Dining

There is a strong French influence in the cuisine of Quebec. However, this province's foods are not the delicate, flavorful dishes traditionally associated with French cuisine. Quebec's food traditions come from ancient, rural France. Meals tend to be heavy and hearty, with lots of meats and starches that keep you filled up and warm during the cold winter days.

A typical breakfast might feature Quebec's famous maple syrup—perhaps served over pancakes, omelets, or fried bananas. A mug of coffee and steamed milk accompanies breakfast. For lunch and dinner, you might have a pork or beef dish, perhaps with a thick soup and side dishes of beans, beets, or other vegetables. With any meal, you are likely to have some of Quebec's excellent baked goods, such as croissants—crescent-shaped rolls of French origin. Desserts in Quebec are often flavored with maple syrup. Maple syrup pie or cakes in maple syrup are common after-dinner treats.

(Continued on next page)

Quebec Food Briefs

Soupe aux pois (French-Canadian Pea Soup)
Quebec is known for its thick, hearty pea soup, which is flavored with salt pork and herbs. For this dish, Quebec cooks often use herbes salées—herbs that have been preserved with salt—instead of fresh or dried herbs. Some versions of this soup include other vegetables, garlic, or a ham bone for extra flavor.

Tourtière (Meat Pie)
The word tourtière comes from the container used in the old days to cook this popular Quebec dish. A tourtière consists of chopped pork, beef, or veal, along with onion and various seasonings, sealed and baked in a flaky pie crust. Although tourtière is a dish traditionally served in French-Canadian homes on Christmas and New Year's Eve, it is also eaten year-round. You can even find these tasty meat pies in the frozen foods aisle of local supermarkets in Quebec and in some New England states.

Poutine
Poutine is a unique version of French fries. This dish can be found in restaurants throughout Quebec—even in fast food chains. Poutine consists of basic french fries, mixed with small chunks of cheese and covered with brown gravy. There are several different versions of this dish, with various cheeses and types of gravies. Turkey or chicken gravies are the most common. Poutine is a relatively new addition to French-Canadian cuisine. According to some sources, it was first created in the 1950s.

Looking Back on Quebec

1. Why might the heavy, rich foods popular in Quebec be less popular in other parts of the world? Do you think they would be popular where you live? Explain your answer.

   _____

   _____

2. Quebec's famous maple syrup comes from the sugar maple tree. Research the maple sugar industry. What products other than maple syrup can be made from sugar maple sap? Present your findings in a report.

   _____

   _____

3. List the foods of Quebec that you would most like to try. Where can you find these foods? Which can you make?

   _____

   _____

4. Some of the dishes of Quebec, such as French-Canadian pea soup, contain high amounts of salt and fat. In the United States, there is an emphasis on eating dishes that are low in total fat and salt. Explain in writing some of the ways you could modify recipes high in salt and fat.

   _____

   _____

British Columbia

At Canada's southwest corner lies the province of British Columbia. British Columbia is the third-largest province in Canada and is about 2 $1/2$ times the size of Japan. Canadian soil ends at British Columbia's southern border, where the states of Washington, Idaho, and Montana begin. British Columbia's west side is bordered partly by the Pacific Ocean and partly by the thin arm of Alaska called the panhandle.

British Columbia is known for its breathtaking scenery. In addition to the majestic Canadian Rocky Mountains on its eastern side, there are the Coastal Mountains along its western coast. This combination of mountains and coastline makes British Columbia—a favorite for sightseers. Between mountain ranges, the province's interior contains tall forests, grasslands, and lakes. British Columbia's climate varies with its geography. The Pacific Coast offers rain and mild temperatures. The interior regions are drier and have more variation in temperature, including very hot summers and very cold winters.

Food Traveler's Notes

Agriculture

Only about 4 percent of British Columbia has land suitable for farming. Where the land is suitable, however, it tends to be very productive. Because the land and climate of British Columbia vary so much, different regions are suitable for producing different crops and livestock. Dairy farming is the province's most important agricultural business. Cattle ranching and poultry farming, however, are also common. In the southern interior regions, farmers grow large crops of tree fruits, berries, and vegetables. Fishing is also a major industry along the coast of this province, which is known for its salmon.

People and Language

Most of the nearly four million people living in British Columbia are descendants of the British. However, the province is also home to one of the largest Chinese communities in North America. There are also a number of other ethnic populations in British Columbia, including Japanese, Filipinos, Indians, Pakistanis, Vietnamese, and Thais. About 80,000 of the inhabitants of British Columbia are native to the land. About half of these native peoples live on reserves. Despite the province's wide variety of ethnic populations, English is the native language of most British Columbians.

Dining

British Columbia's foods and dining customs are influenced by the English heritage of its inhabitants. In some parts of the province, restaurants serve a traditional British high tea in the late afternoon. High tea is served either buffet style or as a sit-down meal. Meat, salad, fruit, scones, and cake are usually part of the high-tea menu along with hot tea, of course! Aside from high tea, meal times and menus in British Columbia are similar to those in the United States. Seafood caught off the coast of British Columbia is especially popular. Visitors are likely to find king crab, oysters, shrimp, cod, and salmon on the lunch or dinner menu, along with locally grown vegetables and fruits.

Tourism is an important part of the economy in British Columbia. The cities of Vancouver and Victoria are major tourist attractions. Favorite destinations are the many ski resorts, campgrounds, and bed-and-breakfast inns. Because there is so much tourism, British Columbia has a large number of restaurants. Some sources say that people in Vancouver dine out more often than the residents of any other city in North America.

(Continued on next page)

British Columbia Food Briefs

Salmon

Visitors to British Columbia have a wide variety of seafood to choose from, but salmon is perhaps the most common. Five different kinds of salmon are caught off the British Columbian coast—spring, coho, chinook, chum, and sockeye. Residents of this province eat their salmon smoked, steamed, pan-fried, breaded, canned, or grilled. This popular fish may be served at breakfast, lunch, or dinner—in spreads, salads, pasta dishes, and omelets.

Fruit

British Columbia is a paradise for fruit lovers! The climate and soil of this province make it one of the most productive fruit-growing regions in the world. Here, farmers grow apples, peaches, pears, prunes, plums, and apricots. Two of the region's most well-known fruits are blueberries and cranberries. British Columbians use these plentiful berries in a wide variety of dishes. Visitors to the region can sample delicious breads and muffins full of fresh berries. They can also try something more unusual. How about chicken grilled in a cranberry sauce and a spinach blueberry salad!

Nanaimo Bars

Nanaimo bars are a traditional Canadian treat. In some parts of Canada, you can find them in every bakery. Although they are popular all throughout the country, Nanaimo Bars originated in the British Columbian city of Nanaimo. There are several variations of the recipe, but they usually have a bottom layer of chocolate, coconut, graham cracker crumbs, and nuts; a middle layer of vanilla custard; and a chocolate icing top.

Looking Back on British Columbia

1. British Columbia is home to a wide variety of ethnic groups. How do you think this ethnic diversity might influence the cuisine of the province? Have ethnic groups had a strong influence on the cuisine in the area in which you live? Explain your answer.

_____

_____

2. Because tourism is a large part of British Columbia's economy, the province has many resorts, hotels, and inns. Using travel guides, find a place in British Columbia that you would like to visit. Research restaurants in that area and list the ones you would like to try. Explain your selection.

_____

_____

3. List the foods of British Columbia that you would most like to try. Where can you find these foods? Which can you make?

_____

_____

4. The foods of British Columbia are similar to those found in the Pacific northwestern areas of the United States. Explain in writing why this might be the case. You may want to include visuals in your report.

_____

_____

U'nega'gei
(Iroquois Fish Soup)

**U'nega'gei
(Iroquois Fish Soup)**

Customary	Ingredients	Metric
2 cups	Chicken broth	500 mL
1 cup	Sliced onion	250 mL
1/4 cup	Sliced mushrooms	50 mL
3 Tbsp.	Cornmeal	45 mL
3 Tbsp.	Chopped parsley	45 mL
1 clove	Minced garlic	1 clove
1/2 tsp.	Basil	2 mL
1/4 tsp.	Salt	1 mL
1/4 tsp.	Pepper	1 mL
12 oz.	White fish fillets, such as haddock or perch	375 g
1 cup	Frozen green beans or baby lima beans	250 mL
1 cup	Chopped fresh spinach	250 mL

Yield: 4 servings

Directions

Pan: 21/2-qt. (2.5-L) saucepan

1. Combine broth, onion, mushrooms, cornmeal, parsley, garlic, basil, salt, and pepper in saucepan. Bring to a boil. Reduce heat and simmer 10 minutes.

2. Cut the fish as needed to fit into the saucepan. Add fish and beans to soup. Simmer 15 minutes longer.

3. Add spinach. Simmer 5 minutes longer.

4. Break fish into bite-size pieces and serve.

Nutrition Information: Serving size: 1/4 recipe

calories: 145
total fat: 2 g
saturated fat: 0 g
cholesterol: 49 mg
sodium: 600 mg

carbohydrate: 12 g
dietary fiber: 3 g
sugars: 2 g
protein: 21 g

Percent Daily Value: vitamin A 18%, vitamin C 20%, calcium 10%, iron 16%

Maple Walnut Tourlouche

Recipe 10

Touring Canada

Maple Walnut Tourlouche

Customary	Ingredients	Metric
3/4 cup	Pure maple syrup	175 mL
1/2 cup	Walnuts, chopped	125 mL
1/2 cup	Raisins	125 mL
1 1/4 cup	All-purpose flour	300 mL
2 tsp.	Baking powder	10 mL
1/4 tsp.	Nutmeg	1 mL
1/8 tsp.	Salt	0.5 mL
1 Tbsp.	Margarine, softened	15 mL
1/4 cup	Sugar	50 mL
1	Egg	1
2/3 cup	Skim milk	150 mL

Yield: 9 servings

Directions

Pan: 1-qt. (1-L) saucepan; 8 x 8 x 2 inch (20 x 20 x 5 cm) baking dish

1. Preheat oven to 350°F (180°C). Grease baking dish.

2. Bring syrup to a boil in saucepan.

3. Pour hot syrup into baking dish. Sprinkle with walnuts and raisins. Set aside and keep warm.

4. Stir together flour, baking powder, nutmeg, and salt. Set aside.

5. Cream margarine and sugar. Beat in egg.

6. Add dry ingredients to creamed mixture alternately with milk, beating well after each addition.

7. Drop batter onto warm syrup by heaping tablespoons, spreading to cover syrup as batter warms.

8. Bake at 350°F (180°C) until golden brown, about 30 minutes.

9. Serve warm from pan or invert onto serving dish.

Nutrition Information: Serving size: 1/9 recipe

calories: 230
total fat: 5 g
saturated fat: 1 g
cholesterol: 24 mg
sodium: 162 mg

carbohydrate: 45 g
dietary fiber: 1 g
sugars: 12 g
protein: 4 g

Percent Daily Value: vitamin A 4%, vitamin C 0%, calcium 6%, iron 9%

Touring Latin America

A Global Foods Tour

The region of the world known as Latin America is made up of all the territory in the Western Hemisphere that is south of the United States and north of Antarctica. Notice on Map 4 (page 19) that the northern tip of Latin America is Mexico. Stretching between the hook-shaped southern part of Mexico and the northwest tip of South America are the countries that make up Central America. In the blue waters of the Caribbean Sea, slightly northeast of Central America, lie the Caribbean Islands. Making up the southernmost part of Latin America is the continent of South America. On Map 5 (page 20), find South America's largest country.

People and Cultures

The countries of Latin America were largely colonized by Spain, Portugal, and France. Because the languages of these countries developed from Latin, the region became known as Latin America. The people of Latin American have a varied heritage. The native people of Mexico and Central America, including the Incas, Mayans, and Aztecs, eventually mixed with the European colonists. The European newcomers also influenced this region's cuisine. Among the foods European settlers introduced to Latin America are chicken, beef, pork, garlic, onions, olive oil, sugar cane, and rice.

Because the colonists imported African slaves into South America and the Caribbean Islands, a population of mixed African and European ancestry developed. Latin American cuisine contains elements of European, African, and Native American cultures, making it a unique blend of three continents.

Cuisines of Latin America

Because of the high cost of meat, most Latin Americans eat very little of it. The people in the cattle-raising countries of Argentina and Uruguay are exceptions. Beef is popular there, but for most Latin Americans, grain is the major food. In tropical areas, the people enjoy bananas, mangoes, oranges, pineapples, and other tropical fruits. Some foods that play an important role in today's Latin American cuisine—such as corn, beans, potatoes, tomatoes, and chili peppers—were eaten centuries ago by native peoples. Chocolate and chilies are two examples of foods eaten today that can be traced to the Aztecs.

The Savvy Gourmet

If you are invited to dinner at a friend's house in Mexico, Brazil, or Panama, no one will be offended if you show up late. In Chile, however, it's a different story. Punctuality is insisted upon in Chilean culture—so be sure to keep an eye on your watch!

Port of Call

Puerto Rico

You only have to travel about 1,000 miles (1,600 km) off the southeast coast of Florida to reach Puerto Rico—one of the islands of Latin America. Puerto Rico forms part of the boundary that separates the Atlantic Ocean from the Caribbean Sea. Sometimes called the Island of Enchantment, Puerto Rico is actually made up of one large island and several smaller ones. Together the islands are not quite three times the size of the state of Rhode Island.

Mountains run east and west through the south-central part of Puerto Rico. The northeastern part of the island is covered with a tropical rain forest. The trade winds, which blow from the east, carry warm air and moisture across the island. The air is almost always warm, and there is little seasonal difference in temperature. The southwestern coastal area receives less rain, however, and has a dry season.

Puerto Rico is a self-governing territory, or commonwealth, of the United States. The people of Puerto Rico are U.S. citizens and can move to the mainland without restrictions. When living on the island, however, they cannot vote in U.S. presidential elections, and they do not pay federal income taxes.

Food Traveler's Notes

Agriculture

Most of Puerto Rico's farms are small and produce foods that are consumed locally. Fewer than 10 percent of all Puerto Rico's farms produce most of the island's agricultural products. The most valuable crop is coffee, followed by vegetables, sugarcane, bananas, pineapples, and rice. Puerto Rican farms also produce dairy products, poultry, and cattle.

People and Language

Approximately 3.5 million people live in Puerto Rico—about 1,000 people per square mile. This population density is higher than almost any state in the United States. Most of the people of Puerto Rico are descended from Spanish colonists. Many Puerto Ricans can also trace their ancestry to Africans and Tainos (natives of the island). Although closely associated with the United States, Puerto Ricans are very loyal to their own heritage, culture, and way of life. Spanish and English are the official languages of the island, but the vast majority of Puerto Ricans speak Spanish.

Dining

Puerto Rican cuisine is somewhat similar to Spanish and Mexican cuisine. However, it has its own style, which is rooted in native cultures and influenced by both the Spanish and African cultures. The diet of the native people of Puerto Rico emphasized corn, seafood, and tropical fruit. Today, Puerto Rican cuisine still contains many native Caribbean foods and flavors, such as the *chayote,* a pear-shaped vegetable similar to summer squash. The Spanish influence is also strong in today's Puerto Rican cuisine. One of the most popular Puerto Rican dishes, chicken soup with rice, would be impossible without the chicken and rice introduced by the Spanish! Several popular foods of Puerto Rico, including okra and the tropical plant taro, can be traced to Africa. The mingling of flavors and techniques from these three cultures is what gives Puerto Rican cooking its character.

(Continued on next page)

Puerto Rican Food Briefs

Plantains

A plantain is a variety of banana that is coarser in texture than ordinary bananas. This fruit is harvested while green, then baked, fried, or boiled—but unlike bananas, plantains cannot be eaten raw. One common way of preparing plantains is to slice and fry them. These are called *tostones* and are usually served as an appetizer. Plantains are also served as a side dish to accompany fish, meat, or poultry dishes. Whichever way they are served, however, plantains are easily one of the most popular foods in Puerto Rico!

Seasonings

Many Puerto Rican foods are flavored by two different seasoning mixtures. *Adobo* is made by crushing together peppercorns, garlic, oregano, salt, olive oil, and vinegar. Cooks coat chicken, fish, and steak with the flavorful adobo a day or so before they are ready to fry, roast, or barbecue. *Sofrito* is a thick liquid seasoning used to flavor beans, soups, and stews. Made of onions, garlic, tomatoes, and peppers, this mixture is sometimes colored with seeds to give it a bright-yellow color.

Desserts

The most common Puerto Rican dessert is called a *flan*. It is a sweet custard. Common versions of this dessert include cream cheese, mashed pumpkin, and coconut. Other traditional desserts include coconut bread pudding and *nisperos de batata,* which are sweet-potato balls with coconut, cloves, and cinnamon. Although coconut is the most common ingredient in desserts, you might also expect to find guava in your dessert. Guava is a tropical fruit, which, depending on the variety, may be sliced and eaten fresh or used to make jams and jellies and to flavor cakes, pies, and other desserts. Papayas and mangoes are other tropical fruits commonly used in Puerto Rican desserts.

Looking Back on Puerto Rico

1. The cuisine of Puerto Rico is a mixture of different cultures. What cultures do you think have influenced the cuisine in your local area? How can this influence be seen? Present your findings in a written report. You may want to include illustrations, samples of restaurant menus in your area, or ads in local newspapers.

2. Imagine that you are planning a trip to Puerto Rico. Research the area and list the sights you would most like to see and the activities you would most like to do. Prepare an itinerary of your trip.

3. Do any of the desserts of Puerto Rico discussed above appeal to you? Which characteristics of the dessert attract you? Why? Share your ideas in a class discussion.

4. If you wanted to try some traditional Puerto Rican cuisine where you live, how would you go about doing so? Where would you find out more? Present your findings to the class.

Port of Call
Mexico

Touring Latin America

The Latin American country of Mexico is nearly three times the size of the state of Texas. Mexico's northern edge borders the southwestern United States. Its far southern tip shares a border with the Central American countries of Belize and Guatemala. The rest of Mexico is bordered by water—the Pacific Ocean on the west and the Gulf of Mexico and the Caribbean Sea on the east. Mexico has two major mountain ranges. One range lies along its eastern edge, the other lies along its western edge. Tucked between the mountain ranges is a large central plateau. Most of Mexico's people live on this plateau.

Northern and central Mexico's climate is generally warm and fairly dry, much like the climate of the southwestern United States. As you travel south, the climate becomes more tropical, with increased rainfall. The extreme southern part of Mexico is rainy, hot, and humid. Much of this region is covered by tropical rain forests.

Food Traveler's Notes

Agriculture
The land in Mexico is not ideal for farming. Almost 80 percent of the country is too mountainous or too dry to produce good crops. Even so, Mexican farms produce almost all the food that is eaten by the Mexican people. The primary food crops are corn and beans, which are staple foods in the Mexican diet. Mexican farmers also grow large crops of tomatoes, coffee, citrus fruits, and sugarcane. Many of these crops are exported to the United States.

People and Language
Approximately 97.5 million people live in Mexico. Almost 80 percent of them are *mestizos,* people of mixed European and Native American ancestry. Most Mexican mestizos have Spanish ancestry, and Spanish is the official language of the country. A number of Native American peoples also live in Mexico, mostly in the southern parts of the country. As many as 100 Native American languages are still spoken in Mexico.

Many Mexican foods have become part of the vocabulary and part of the cuisine in other Latin American countries, the United States, and elsewhere. Two examples are *tortillas*—pancakes made of corn flour—and *tacos*—folded tortillas filled with meats, avocado, beans, vegetables, and spicy sauce.

Dining
Mexicans usually eat their main meal, which is called comida, in the afternoons, between 1:00 and 4:00 P.M. This is the traditional siesta time, when many businesses close and people go home for their family meals. The evening meal is eaten around 9:00 P.M., and often consists of a light snack and a cup of hot chocolate.

Although Mexican food has a reputation for being hot and spicy, most traditional dishes are mild. Mexican cooks often serve a spicy sauce on the side, however, for those who like their foods hot. The Mexican word for hot is *caliente,* but this word refers to actual heat. The word for *spicy* is *picante*. If you want to know if something is spicy, ask *"Es picante?"*

(Continued on next page)

Port of Call: Mexico (continued)

Mexican Food Briefs

Tortillas

Tortillas—thin pancakes made of corn flour—are one of the best known and most important traditional Mexican foods. They are a part of nearly every Mexican meal, much as bread is a part of many American meals. Although some Mexican cooks make their own tortillas at home, tortilla bakeries are very common in Mexican cities. In the United States, both wheat-flour tortillas and corn-flour tortillas are sold. If you visit Mexico, don't expect to find many wheat-flour tortillas on the menu. True Mexican tortillas are almost always made out of corn flour.

Chilies

Mexico is home to more than 100 varieties of chili peppers. Although chilies are widely known for being spicy hot, different varieties have different flavors and levels of spiciness. Hotter chilies include the *habanero, serrano,* and *jalapeno*. Other chilies, such as the *anaheim* and *poblano,* are much milder. Some have a sweet, nutty, or smoky flavor. Chilies are essential ingredients in Mexican cuisine and are sold, both fresh and dried, in most Mexican markets. Cooks know just which chilies add the best flavor to a dish.

Mole

Mole (moh-lay) is a rich, dark reddish-brown sauce traditional to Mexican cuisine. The word comes from a Native American word *molli,* which means a concoction. There are many kinds of moles, but most are a blend of onion, garlic, different chilies, ground nuts or seeds, and a small amount of chocolate. Some moles also contain turkey, chicken, and various vegetables. Mole may be eaten as a sauce served over poultry dishes or as a stewlike main dish.

Looking Back on Mexico

1. If you decided to take your main meal between 1:00 and 4:00 in the afternoon, as the Mexicans do, what changes would you have to make to your daily schedule? Would it be possible? Prepare a report about why it would or would not be possible.

2. There are many regional food specialties in Mexico. Use cookbooks or travel guides to research one region of the country and write down what the people of that region like to eat.

3. List the foods of Mexico that you would most like to try. Where can you find these foods? Which can you make?

4. The Americanized version of Mexican food is often quite different from traditional Mexican food. Research or sample some Mexican food in your area and explain whether and how it differs from the traditional Mexican foods you have read about.

Rollos de Coco

Rollos de Coco
(Coconut Logs)

Customary	Ingredients	Metric
4	Plantains, very ripe, peeled and halved lengthwise	4
1/4 cup	Margarine or butter, melted	50 mL
2 Tbsp.	Brown sugar	30 mL
1 1/2 Tbsp.	Lemon juice	22 mL
1 tsp.	Vanilla flavoring (optional)	5 mL
1/2 cup	Coconut, shredded	125 mL
	Nutmeg to taste	

Yield: 4 servings

Directions

Pan: Baking dish

1. Place plantains in greased baking dish.

2. Combine melted margarine or butter, brown sugar, lemon juice, and vanilla flavoring (if desired).

3. Pour margarine mixture over plantains. Sprinkle with coconut and nutmeg.

4. Bake at 425°F (220°C) until plantains are tender, 20 to 25 minutes. Serve warm.

Nutrition Information: Serving size: 1/4 recipe

calories: 384
total fat: 15 g
saturated fat: 5 g
cholesterol: 0 mg
sodium: 143 mg

carbohydrate: 66 g
dietary fiber: 1 g
sugars: 7 g
protein: 3 g

Percent Daily Value: vitamin A 42%, vitamin C 59%, calcium 2%, iron 10%

Tips for Success

◆ Plantains resemble bananas, but they are larger and have a firm, starchy texture. Very ripe plantains often have a black skin.

Tamales

Tamales
(Mexican Main Dish)

Customary	Ingredients	Metric
24	Fresh corn husks	24
1/4 cup	Vegetable shortening	50 mL
1 cup	Finely ground cornmeal	250 mL
1 tsp.	Baking powder	5 mL
1/2 tsp.	Salt	2 mL
3/4 cup	Chicken broth	175 mL
3/4 cup	Mole Poblano (Recipe 13), or other choice of filling	175 mL

Yield: 12 tamales

Directions

Pans: Steamer basket or colander; saucepan with tight-fitting cover

1. Trim tops and bottoms of husks to form flat ends. Soak husks 5 minutes in hot water; drain.

2. Cream shortening using high-speed electric mixer until very fluffy, about 5 minutes.

3. Combine cornmeal, baking powder, and salt. Gradually beat in shortening until well combined.

4. Add chicken broth slowly, beating constantly, until a small ball of dough is light enough to float in a glass of cold water.

5. Lay out two corn husks, overlapping the edges, to form a 4 x 9 inch (10 x 23 cm) rectangle.

6. Spread about 1 Tbsp. (15 mL) dough into 3 x 4 inch (7.5 x 10 cm) rectangle in the center of the husks.

7. Drop about 1 Tbsp. (15 mL) filling onto the center of the dough.

8. Fold long sides of husks toward center, overlapping the ends. Repeat with shorter sides to form a small bundle. Tie with string.

9. Repeat Steps 5-8 with remaining husks, dough, and filling.

10. Place tamales in layers, seam side down, in a flat-bottomed steamer basket or colander. Place over boiling water in a tightly covered pan. Steam until dough is completely cooked, about one hour.

11. Remove string and husks before eating.

Nutrition Information: Serving size: 3 tamales with Mole Poblano Filling

calories: 243
total fat: 15 g
saturated fat: 3 g

cholesterol: 3 mg
sodium: 527 mg
carbohydrate: 25 g

dietary fiber: 5 g
sugars: 0.2 g
protein: 2 g

Percent Daily Value: vitamin A 1%, vitamin C 1%, calcium 0.5%, iron 8%

Mole Poblano

Mole Poblano
(Turkey in a Mexican Sauce)

Customary	Ingredients	Metric
1/4 cup	Almonds, slivered	50 mL
2 Tbsp.	Sesame seeds	30 mL
1 medium	Tomato	1 medium
4-oz. can	Green chilies, drained	125-g can
2 Tbsp.	Raisins	30 mL
1 Tbsp.	Flour	15 mL
1/2 tsp.	Ground cinnamon	2 mL
1/4 tsp.	Pepper	1 mL
1/8 tsp.	Anise seed	0.5 mL
1/8 tsp.	Ground cloves	0.5 mL
2 cups	Chicken broth	500 mL
2 Tbsp.	Vegetable oil	30 mL
1 medium	Onion, diced	1 medium
1 clove	Garlic, minced	1 clove
1 lb.	Boneless, skinless turkey, cut into strips	500 g
1/2 oz.	Unsweetened chocolate	14 g

Yield: 4 servings

Directions

Pan: Large skillet

1. Toast almonds and sesame seeds in dry skillet over low heat, stirring often, until lightly browned.

2. Put almonds, sesame seeds, tomato, chilies, raisins, flour, cinnamon, pepper, anise seed, cloves, and broth in blender. Cover and blend until smooth.

3. Heat vegetable oil in skillet. Add onion and garlic; sauté until softened.

4. Add turkey pieces to skillet and brown on all sides.

5. Slowly add seasoned broth from blender to turkey mixture. Bring to a boil. Reduce heat, cover, and simmer until turkey is tender, about 10 minutes.

6. Add chocolate. Stir over low heat until chocolate is melted.

7. Serve over rice, or dice meat finely and use as filling for Tamales (Recipe 12).

Nutrition Information: Serving size: 1/4 recipe

calories: 415	cholesterol: 87 mg	dietary fiber: 3 g
total fat: 21 g	sodium: 807 mg	sugars: 7 g
saturated fat: 4 g	carbohydrate: 17 g	protein: 40 g

Percent Daily Value: vitamin A 44%, vitamin C 47%, calcium 14%, iron 27%

Ceviche

Ceviche
(Peruvian Marinated Fish)

Customary	Ingredients	Metric
1 lb.	Firm white fish fillets	500 g
2/3 cup	Lemon juice	150 mL
1/2 cup	Lime juice	125 mL
1	Red pepper, diced	1
1	Green pepper, diced	1
1 small	Onion, chopped	1 small
1 clove	Garlic, minced	1 clove
1/4 tsp.	Salt	1 mL
1/8 tsp.	Pepper	0.5 mL
2 Tbsp.	Cilantro, chopped	30 mL
4 leaves	Romaine lettuce	4 leaves

Yield: about 24 appetizers

Directions

Pan: Skillet (or microwave-safe baking dish)

1. Place fish fillets in skillet with enough water to cover. Bring water to a boil. Reduce heat and simmer, covered, 10 to 12 minutes or until fish flakes easily with a fork. (Or place fish in baking dish; cover. Microwave at 100% power for 3 to 6 minutes. Let stand 5 minutes.)

2. Refrigerate fish until chilled.

3. Cut fillets into cubes. Place in deep dish or bowl. Combine lemon and lime juice, red and green pepper, onion, garlic, salt, pepper, and cilantro; pour over fish.

4. Cover and refrigerate fish mixture overnight.

5. Drain fish. Skewer fish cubes on toothpicks and arrange on lettuce leaves.

Nutrition Information: Serving Size: 1 appetizer

calories: 24
total fat: 0 g
saturated fat: 0 g
cholesterol: 8 mg
sodium: 34 mg

carbohydrate: 2 g
dietary fiber: 0 g
sugars: 0.5 g
protein: 4 g

Percent Daily Value: vitamin A 0%, vitamin C 19%, calcium 1%, iron 1%

Tips for Success

• Traditional ceviche is made with raw fish. Poaching the fish ensures it is safe to eat.

Chayotes Rellenos con Queso

(Chayotes Stuffed with Cheese)

Chayotes Rellenos con Queso
(Chayotes Stuffed with Cheese)

Customary	Ingredients	Metric
2	Chayotes, halved and seeded	2
1 small	Onion, chopped	1 small
1 1/2 Tbsp.	Margarine or butter*	22 mL
1/2 tsp.	Salt	2 mL
1/4 tsp.	Pepper	1 mL
1	Egg, slightly beaten	1
1/3 cup	Monterey Jack cheese, shredded	75 mL
1/3 cup	Fresh bread crumbs	75 mL

Yield: 4 servings

Conventional Directions

Pans: Medium saucepan; baking pan

1. Cook chayotes in boiling water until tender, about 45 minutes.

2. Scoop out pulp from chayotes, being careful not to tear the shells. Mash pulp in a bowl. Set shells and pulp aside.

3. Melt butter or margarine in saucepan. Sauté onion until translucent, about 3 minutes.

4. Add chayote pulp, salt, and pepper. Cook and stir 2 to 3 minutes longer.

5. Remove from heat. Stir in egg and cheese.

6. Fill chayote shells with pulp mixture. Top filled shells with bread crumbs.

7. Place filled shells in greased baking pan. Bake at 350°F (180°C) until crumbs are golden brown, 20 to 25 minutes.

8. Serve chayotes in the shell. Discard shell after eating filling.

(Continued on next page)

Recipe 15 Chayotes (continued)

Microwave Directions

Pan: Microwave-safe baking dish

*Ingredients: Replace margarine or butter with water

1. Place chayotes, cut side down, in baking dish. Cover with waxed paper. Microwave at 100% power for 8 minutes.

2. Turn chayotes cut side up. Microwave at 100% power for 3 to 5 minutes. Let stand, covered, about 5 minutes.

3. Scoop out pulp from chayotes, being careful not to tear the shells. Mash pulp in a bowl. Set shells and pulp aside.

4. Combine onions and water in baking dish. Microwave at 100% power for 1 to 2 minutes or until onions are translucent.

5. Add chayote pulp, salt, pepper, egg, and cheese. Mix well. Fill chayote shells with pulp mixture.

6. Place filled shell in baking dish. Microwave at 50% power for 4 minutes.

7. Top filled shells with bread crumbs. Rotate dish. Microwave at 50% power for 2 to 4 minutes.

8. Let stand, covered, 5 minutes.

9. Serve chayotes in the shell. Discard shell after eating filling.

Nutrition Information: Serving size: ¹/₄ recipe

calories: 135
total fat: 8 g
saturated fat: 2 g
cholesterol: 59 mg
sodium: 399 mg

carbohydrate: 12 g
dietary fiber: 3 g
sugars: 4 g
protein: 6 g

Percent Daily Value: vitamin A 14%, vitamin C 16%, calcium 7%, iron 6%

Tips for Success

◆ Chayotes (chy-OH-tays) are tropical gourds native to Central America. They are pear-shaped with a bumpy green skin. They have a flavor similar to zucchini. You can prepare them as you would any summer squash.

Touring Southern Europe

A Global Foods Tour

Find France, Italy, Spain, and Portugal on Map 6 (page 21). These countries, which combined are slightly larger than twice the size of the state of Texas, make up the southern part of Western Europe. More than 165 million people live here. Southern Europe is nearly surrounded by water and includes two peninsulas—the Iberian Peninsula, made up of Spain and Portugal, and the long, skinny boot-shaped peninsula that is Italy. The region also contains the French island of Corsica, the Italian islands of Sardinia and Sicily, and the Spanish Canary Islands and Balearic Islands.

Packing for a trip to Southern Europe takes careful planning because of the wide range of climates you might find. The region offers a little bit of everything, from cold and dry to mild and moist. The warm waters of the Mediterranean Sea, which seldom drop below 40°F (4°C), are the source of much of the mild climate of Southern Europe. This Mediterranean climate is especially suitable for growing wheat, olives, grapes, and citrus fruits—the crops for which Southern Europe is known.

People and Cultures

The cultures of Southern Europe differ from country to country. In France and Spain, the majority of people live in cities. The country of Portugal, however, is mostly rural, and most Portuguese live in small country villages. In Italy, two-thirds of the population live in the industrial, northern part, where such major cities, as Rome and Florence are. The southern part of Italy is primarily agricultural, and the people there mostly live on farms or in small villages.

Cuisines of Southern Europe

Southern Europe is home to some of the world's most famous cuisines. Italian cuisine is especially well known for its pastas and sauces. Olive oil, tomatoes, garlic, basil, and oregano are common ingredients in Italian foods. Because seafood is more plentiful than beef in Italy, many Italian dishes feature fish or shellfish. In Spain and Portugal, as in Italy, many dishes contain tomatoes, garlic, and onions. In these countries, however, many foods are flavored with a yellow spice called saffron. French cuisine is known for its flavorful sauces, cheeses, and pastries. Because its climate is well-suited for growing grapes, France also has some of the world's most famous vineyards.

The Savvy Gourmet

Native Southern Europeans eat in continental style. To follow this style, hold your fork in your left hand and your knife in your right hand. As you eat, don't switch either utensil to the opposite hand. When you finish eating, place your flatware side by side on your plate. In Spain, crossing the knife and fork means you want more to eat!

Port of Call

Spain

Spain is home to nearly 40 million people. With an area about the size of the states of Colorado and Wyoming combined, Spain is the third largest country in Europe. Portugal and France are the only countries that border Spain; the rest of Spanish soil ends at water's edge—at the Atlantic Ocean on the north and northeast and the Mediterranean Sea on the east and south. The Pyrenees Mountains separate Spain from France and the rest of Europe. Tourists to Spain have a variety of geographical features to visit including mountains, plains, and beaches.

The climate of Spain is also varied. There are four general climate zones. The mildest and most temperate zone is the Mediterranean climate of Spain's south and southeastern regions. Much of this area can count on at least 320 days of sunshine a year. This is the part of Spain that is home to bullfights; to the foot-stamping, heel-clicking, hand-clapping flamenco dancers; and to gazpacho, the famous chilled summer soup made of pureed vegetables, tomatoes, hot chilies, and vinegar. For many, this is the area that the name *Spain* brings to mind.

Food Traveler's Notes

Agriculture

Spain is one of Europe's leading fishing countries—mussels, sardines, cod, anchovies, and squid are major catches. The chief agriculture products include barley, milk, olives, oranges, potatoes, tomatoes, and wheat. However, Spain's generally poor soil combined with its dry climate in most regions results in low agricultural production. Sheep are the chief livestock of Spain.

People and Language

The official language of Spain is Spanish—most often called Castilian or *Castellano* by Spaniards. Regional languages include Catalán, in Catalonia; Galician, in the northwest; and Basque in the northern Basque provinces. In these regions, it is not uncommon to find menus, street signs, and other printed material in the regional language.

Several foods and food names that have become commonplace in the United States and other countries can be traced back to Spain. *Salsa,* a spicy condiment made of tomatoes, onions, and hot peppers, originated in Spain. The word *caramel* is of Spanish origin, and caramel sauce is a favorite topping for the egg custard that is often served at the end of Spanish meals. The Spanish explorers of the 1500s are credited with bringing back to Europe potatoes, which originally grew in the Andes Mountains of South America. The English word *potato* was taken from the Spanish word *papata,* which was a variation of the South American Indian word *batata.*

Dining

A typical Spanish breakfast consists of sweet, thick hot chocolate and *churros,* which are fried donuts. The midday meal is usually served between 1:00 P.M. and 3:30 P.M. The peak time for lunch is about 2:00 P.M. A Spanish lunch usually has four courses. It might begin with soup or hors d'oeuvres. An egg or fish dish might come next and is followed by meat and vegetables. Nearly all businesses in Spain close during the lunch period, usually shutting down between 1:00 P.M. and 4:30 P.M. and then remaining open until 8:00 P.M. or so. In the early evening, people often snack on tapas, which are small finger-food snacks. (See Spanish Food Briefs.) Eating tapas takes the edge off appetites until dinner, which is served between 9:30 and 11:00 P.M. Like lunch, dinner is another four or five course meal.

(Continued on next page)

Name _____ Date _____ Class _____## Spanish Food Briefs

Paella

If Spain has a signature dish, it is probably *paella.* First prepared about 200 years ago in the region of Valencia, paella is named for the two-handled metal pan in which it is traditionally cooked and served. The ingredients of paella include chicken, red peppers, shellfish, peas, and sometimes snails. All of these are served on a bed of saffron-flavored rice.

Tapas

Many countries, including the United States, have welcomed Spanish *tapas* into their restaurant cuisine. Tapas are snacks or appetizers that you can eat with your fingers or with a toothpick. Tapas cafés are now found in most Spanish cities, but the southern region of Andalusia is thought to be the place where tapas originated. The word *tapas* means a cover or a lid. The first tapas was probably a thin slice of sausage or ham that was placed over the mouth of a glass to keep flies out. Today, tapas include olives, toasted almonds, and other simple snacks, as well as food combinations, such as veal rolls, stuffed peppers, and peppery octopus.

Desserts

Desserts are not emphasized in Spanish restaurant menus, and, in general, Spain does not seem to worry much about satisfying a sweet tooth. *Flan,* an egg custard, is a standby on most restaurant menus, and ice cream may be the only other choice. An item that many tourists are surprised to find on some dessert menus is a glass of fresh orange juice.

Looking Back on Spain

1. If the people in your area decided to adopt a meal schedule and pattern like that of Spain, what other changes would have to be made? Do you think you would like this new arrangement? Explain your answer.

2. Use travel guides to research a city in Spain that you might like to visit. List the places or things that you would like to see. Look through the restaurant descriptions and choose places in which you would like to eat. Imagine that you have spent a day as a tourist in the city you have researched. Write a diary entry describing how you spent one full day.

3. List the foods of Spain that you would most like to try. Where can you find these foods? Which can you make?

4. Today tapas include a variety of foods and food combinations. Invent a snack that you think would appeal to customers of a restaurant in your area. Explain why you think your snack qualifies as tapas and why it might appeal to people in your area.

Port of Call

France

France lies on the west coast of the European mainland. It is bordered on the north by the English Channel, which separates it from England. The European countries of Belgium, Germany, Switzerland, and Italy lie along France's eastern borders. At the bottom of the country are the Pyrenees Mountains, which divide France from Spain, its neighbor to the southwest. Along the southeast edge of France is the Mediterranean Sea and the famous resort area known as the French Riviera. France is a little more than 210,000 square miles (546,000 square km)—approximately twice the size of the state of Colorado.

Much of France has a moderate, comfortable climate with cool winters and mild summers. However, this is not the case in every region. In the semitropical climate of the Mediterranean coast, for example, winters are mild and summers are quite hot. In the northeastern regions, near Belgium and Germany, winters can be severe.

Food Traveler's Notes

Agriculture

One of France's most famous agricultural products is grapes. Millions of grapes are grown and harvested every year in the fertile river valleys of central France. Other important French agricultural products include wheat, sugar beets, potatoes, dairy products, and beef cattle.

People and Language

More than 58 million people call France home. Almost three-fourths of them live in the larger cities, such as Paris, Marseilles, and Lyon. More than 90 percent of the people living in France are native-born French, but there are also ethnic groups of Portuguese, Algerians, Moroccans, Italians, and Turks.

French is the only official language of France, and the majority of people speak it. In some areas, several regional languages are also spoken. For example, people in Bretagne speak a language called *Breton.* People of Provence speak *Provençal,* and people in the Pyrenees region speak *Basque* and *Catalan.*

Dining

The French are famous for their cuisine, and they take it very seriously! There are three categories of French cuisine. *Haute cuisine* is perhaps the most famous category. In haute cuisine, cooking is considered an art form. Usually found in famous restaurants, haute cuisine meals may take hours to prepare and are often presented elaborately. The second category, *cuisine bourgeoise,* refers to French home cooking. The third category, *nouvelle cuisine,* is a lighter style of cooking designed to preserve the natural flavors of ingredients. Nouvelle cuisine is the newest style of French cuisine. It began in the 1970s.

Whatever the cuisine, the French take great pleasure in their meals. As a rule, they eat three meals a day. Breakfasts are usually light, consisting of coffee and bread or pastries. Lunches and dinners frequently have several courses and are usually eaten at a relaxed pace. Many businesses close for two hours in the middle of the day for the lunch break.

(Continued on next page)

French Food Briefs

Sauces

Sauces are featured in French cuisine. There are dozens of French sauces; each is made from a special combination of a variety of ingredients. Served on meat, poultry, eggs, and vegetables, the sauce is often the part of a French dish that gives it its unique flavor. Many French sauces begin with a *roux,* which is simply butter and flour cooked together. To make a sauce, you add milk, cream, broth, or other ingredients to the roux. Some French sauces, including béarnaise, mayonnaise, and hollandaise, use egg yolks and butter for a base.

Cheese

The French often serve cheese by itself as one of the courses in their meals—and with good reason! France is famous for its delicious cheeses, and there are hundreds of local cheeses from which to choose. French cheeses vary from region to region. The kind of cheese a region offers is influenced by many factors including the particular cows or goats whose milk is used to make the cheese. The type of fields in which they graze and the length of the day also contribute to the flavor of the cheese. Of the many different kinds of French cheeses, some of the most famous are *Brie, Camembert,* and *Roquefort.* French cheeses are often named after the towns or regions where they are made.

Regional Cuisines

Many parts of France are known for their regional cooking styles and specialty dishes. These regional specialties often include foods that are grown or raised locally. For example, meals along the Mediterranean coast often feature the seafood and olive oil that are common there. Beef from the cattle raised in the Burgundy region of central France appears frequently in recipes in this area. Beef Burgundy is one famous dish from this region. Regional cooking styles are sometimes also influenced by neighboring countries. In the eastern parts of France, the German culture influences cuisine. Here, you will find dishes featuring the sauerkraut and pork sausages common in German meals.

Looking Back on France

1. Research the process of making cheese. Write a brief paragraph describing the main steps of the process.

2. The French classify cuisine into three categories. Do you think there are categories of cuisine in the area where you live? Explain your answer.

3. List the foods of France that you would most like to try. Where can you find these foods? Which can you make?

4. Sauces are one of the most important parts of many French dishes. Imagine that you are creating a sauce based on a simple flour-and-butter roux. What ingredients would you add for flavor? Which foods would your sauce complement? Write an article for a foods magazine describing your sauce.

Tortilla de Patatas
(Potato Omelet of Spain)

Tortilla de Patatas
(Potato Omelet of Spain)

Customary	Ingredients	Metric
1/4 cup	Olive oil	50 mL
8 oz.	Potatoes, quartered and thinly sliced	250 g
1/2 cup	Onion, thinly sliced	125 mL
2 cloves	Garlic, minced	2 cloves
5	Eggs	5
1/2 tsp.	Salt	2 mL
1/4 tsp.	Pepper	1 mL

Yield: 4 servings

Conventional Directions

Pan: Large skillet

1. Heat oil in skillet. When hot, carefully add potatoes and fry until light brown, turning often. To avoid hot oil spatter, make sure potatoes are dry before adding to oil.

2. Add onion and garlic. Cook over low heat, turning potatoes often, until potatoes are tender, about 10 minutes.

3. Remove skillet from heat. Transfer potatoes to a large bowl. Reserve oil.

4. Beat eggs with salt and pepper until frothy. Carefully stir eggs into potatoes.

5. Return skillet to heat. Spread egg mixture evenly in skillet.

6. Cook over medium heat until omelet is firm but not dry, 5 to 7 minutes. Shake skillet frequently to prevent sticking.

7. Place large plate upside down over skillet. Invert skillet and omelet onto plate. Slide omelet back into skillet, uncooked side down. Cook about 2 minutes longer.

Microwave Directions

Pan: 9-inch (23-cm) microwave-safe glass pie pan

1. Pour oil into pie pan. Add potatoes and stir to coat.

2. Microwave at 100 percent power for 3 minutes.

3. Stir in onions and garlic, spreading mixture evenly in pan. Microwave at 100 percent power for 4 minutes or until potatoes are tender.

4. Beat eggs with salt and pepper. Pour over potato mixture. Cover with waxed paper.

5. Microwave at 100 percent power just until center is set, about 5 minutes, rotating pan every 1 1/2 minutes.

6. Let stand 3 minutes before serving.

Nutrition Information: Serving size: 1/4 recipe

calories: 285	carbohydrate: 17 g
total fat: 20 g	dietary fiber: 2 g
saturated fat: 4 g	sugars: 1 g
cholesterol: 266 mg	protein: 9 g
sodium: 351 mg	

Percent Daily Value: vitamin A 14%, vitamin C 15%, calcium 5%, iron 12%

Ratatouille

(Vegetable Stew of France)

Ratatouille
(Vegetable Stew of France)

Customary	Ingredients	Metric
1/2 cup	Thinly sliced onion	125 mL
1 clove	Minced garlic	1 clove
1/4 cup	Olive oil	50 mL
1 1/2 cups	Green pepper strips	350 mL
2 cups	Cubed eggplant	500 mL
2 cups	Sliced zucchini	500 mL
1 1/2 cups	Peeled, seeded tomato chunks	350 mL
1 tsp.	Basil	5 mL
1/2 tsp.	Oregano	2 mL
1/4 tsp.	Salt	1 mL
1/8 tsp.	Pepper	0.5 mL

Yield: 4 servings

Directions

Pan: Large skillet

1. Heat oil in skillet. Sauté onion and garlic in oil for about 3 minutes.

2. Add green pepper. Cook, stirring occasionally, about 5 minutes longer.

3. Stir in eggplant and zucchini. Simmer, covered, about 20 minutes.

4. Add tomato, basil, oregano, salt, and pepper. Stir gently. Cover and continue simmering until mixture is thick and vegetables are soft, about 15 minutes.

Nutrition Information: Serving size: 1/4 recipe

calories: 175
total fat: 14 g
saturated fat: 2 g
cholesterol: 0 mg
sodium: 284 mg

carbohydrate: 12 g
dietary fiber: 4 g
sugars: 6 g
protein: 3 g

Percent Daily Value: vitamin A 11%, vitamin C 63%, calcium 6%, iron 9%

Tips for Success

◆ If the mixture is too watery near the end of cooking, remove the cover and simmer until the excess liquid has evaporated.

Polenta con Salsa di Pomodoro

(Italian Cornmeal Dish with Tomato Sauce)

Recipe 18

Touring Southern Europe

Polenta con Salsa di Pomodoro
(Italian Cornmeal Dish with Tomato Sauce)

Customary	Ingredients	Metric
4 cups	Water	1 L
1 tsp.	Salt	5 mL
1 cup	Yellow cornmeal	250 mL
	Salsa di Pomodoro (recipe follows)	

Yield: 4 servings

Directions

Pan: 2-qt. (2-L) saucepan

1. Combine water and salt in saucepan. Bring to a rolling boil.

2. Reduce heat to a gentle boil. Gradually add cornmeal, stirring constantly.

3. Cook, stirring constantly, until mixture becomes very thick, about 20 minutes.

4. Immediately turn mixture out onto large platter or board. Cool until set, about 3 minutes.

5. Slice polenta and serve with Salsa di Pomodoro.

Tips for Success

◆ Traditionally, polenta is sliced by wrapping a string around the desired portion. The ends of the string are then pulled in opposite directions until it has cut through the polenta.

(Continued on next page)

Recipe 18 Polenta con Salsa di Pomodoro (continued)

Salsa di Pomodoro
(Tomato Sauce)

Customary	Ingredients	Metric
2 Tbsp.	Margarine or butter	30 mL
2 Tbsp.	Olive oil	30 mL
1/3 cup	Sliced onion	75 mL
Two 8-oz. cans	Tomato sauce	Two 250-g cans
1 cup	Beef broth	250 mL
1 cup	Peeled, seeded tomato chunks	250 mL
1 tsp.	Basil	5 mL
1/2 tsp.	Oregano	2 mL
1/2 tsp.	Rosemary	2 mL

Yield: About 2$1/2$ cups (625 mL)

Directions

Pan: 1-qt. (1-L) saucepan

1. Heat margarine or butter and olive oil over low heat. Add onion and sauté for about 3 minutes.

2. Add tomato sauce and beef broth. Bring to a boil.

3. Reduce heat to simmer. Stir in tomato chunks.

4. Simmer sauce about 20 minutes.

5. Stir in basil, oregano, and rosemary. Simmer 15 minutes longer.

6. Serve over polenta.

Nutrition Information: Serving size: 1/4 of polenta with 1/4 cup (50 mL) sauce

calories: 171
total fat: 6 g
saturated fat: 1 g
cholesterol: 0 mg
sodium: 714 mg

carbohydrate: 27 g
dietary fiber: 2 g
sugars: 1 g
protein: 4 g

Percent Daily Value: vitamin A 15%, vitamin C 12%, calcium 3%, iron 10%

Touring Northern Europe

A Global Foods Tour

Washed by the waters of the Baltic and North Seas are the countries of Northern Europe—Finland, Germany, Ireland, the United Kingdom, and the Scandinavian countries of Norway, Sweden, and Denmark. To find these countries on Map 6 (see page 21), first locate and mark the Baltic and North Seas.

In the varied geography of Northern Europe, there are miles and miles of coastline, narrow fjords, snow-covered mountains, flat lowlands, and fruit-bearing river valleys. Together, the countries of Northern Europe make up almost 700,000 square miles (1,726,652 square km) of land.

Although the countries of Northern Europe are relatively close to the Arctic Circle, the climate in most of this region is surprisingly mild. The island nations of Ireland and the United Kingdom tend to be damp and overcast much of the time. Norway, too, gets a fair amount of rainfall. Toward the northern tips of Norway, Sweden, and Finland, the climate becomes much colder than the rest of Northern Europe.

People and Language

Approximately 167 million people live in the countries of Northern Europe. Almost half live in the highly populated nation of Germany. The United Kingdom contains another third of the total Northern European population. Not surprisingly, the two most common languages are German, which is spoken in Germany, and English, which is spoken in the United Kingdom and Ireland. Each Scandinavian country has its own language.

Cuisines of Northern Europe

Northern Europe has a wide range of food resources, and the visitor to this region can expect plenty of good, filling meals. While food choices differ from country to country, Northern European cuisines in general are fairly simple—sometimes called "meat and potatoes" cuisines. Seafood, pork, beef, poultry, and lamb are plentiful in this region. The meat and seafood are featured in the hearty stews, sausages, and roasts that are common main dishes in Northern European cultures. Dairy products, breads, potatoes, and a wide range of other vegetables round out Northern European food choices.

The Savvy Gourmet

Because the growing season in Scandinavian countries is short, meals are often low in fresh fruits and vegetables. You may, however, be served fuksoppa, a soup of dried fruit and tapioca cooked in a sweetened liquid. Don't expect to get warmed up by this soup—fuksoppa is served cold!

Port of Call

United Kingdom

The official name for the United Kingdom, or the UK, is the *United Kingdom of Great Britain and Northern Ireland*. The largest part of the United Kingdom is the island of Great Britain, which lies just across the English Channel from France. Great Britain is made up of Scotland, Wales, and England. Much of the island is mountainous, especially in Scotland and Wales. England takes up most of the southern part of Great Britain—famous for London, Shakespeare, and afternoon tea, among many other things. When you mention the UK to many people, England is what comes to mind.

Northern Ireland makes up the second and smaller part of the United Kingdom. Northern Ireland is located in the northeastern corner of the island of Ireland. Unlike the rest of the United Kingdom, Northern Ireland is mostly flat. The climate throughout the United Kingdom is mild and damp. Fog, mist, and overcast skies are common.

Food Traveler's Notes

Agriculture

Much of the land in Great Britain is not suitable for farming. Therefore, the nation has to import more than half of its food from other countries. Livestock and dairy products are more important than field crops in Great Britain's agriculture. Fishing is also an important industry, especially in Scotland. The land in Northern Ireland is more fertile than the land in Great Britain. Livestock, potatoes, and grains are some of Northern Ireland's agricultural products.

People and Language

There are more than 57.5 million people living in the United Kingdom, making it very densely populated. To get an idea of how crowded this small island nation is, consider that the state of Oregon—which is approximately the same size—has fewer than three million people. Almost 90 percent of the total population of the United Kingdom live in cities. The UK's largest city, London, has a population of 6.8 million.

English is the most commonly spoken language of Great Britain. However, about one-fourth of the people who live in Wales speak Welsh, and a small segment of Scottish people speak a Gaelic language. Most people who live in Northern Ireland have Scottish or English ancestry and are called "Scotch-Irish." Here, English is the only official language.

Dining

Visitors to the United Kingdom can expect to greet the day with a hearty meal. A typical breakfast might include hot or cold cereal, fruit, eggs, and a "fry-up" of bacon, sausage, kidney, mushrooms, and tomatoes—and, of course toast and jam! Lunch is usually between noon and 2:00 P.M. and is also fairly heavy. This meal often consists of a meat stew and two vegetables, followed by dessert. The Sunday midday meal is especially important in the United Kingdom. This large meal traditionally features a roast—called a joint—of beef, lamb, or pork.

In Great Britain, late afternoon is teatime. This small meal often includes sandwiches, tea cakes, or cookies, in addition to hot tea and thick cream. Supper, the final meal of the day, is usually eaten between 6:00 and 7:00 P.M. Supper is a lighter meal than lunch, often followed by cheese, crackers, and coffee.

(Continued on next page)

United Kingdom Food Briefs

Puddings

People of the United Kingdom use the word "pudding" to refer to several different kinds of dishes. Historically, the British made puddings by stuffing a mixture of ingredients into the stomach bag or intestines of an animal and boiling it. Fortunately for cooks, most English puddings today are made in a bowl! Many puddings are desserts, made of milk or cream, eggs, and sometimes fruit. Other puddings, however, are side dishes. Yorkshire pudding, which is typically served with roast beef, is a light, fluffy popover-like mixture cooked in the beef drippings from the roasting pan.

Fish

Fish are an important part of many meals in the United Kingdom. Visitors to the UK can expect to find flounder, halibut, sole, haddock, cod, mackerel, sardines, or herring on the lunch or dinner menu. Some British people even eat fish for breakfast! One of the most famous is the kipper—a salt-cured, smoked herring. Kippers can either be eaten alone or used as an ingredient in a recipe.

Scones

No British tea is complete without scones—small, rich breads in a variety of shapes. According to one legend, scones are named after the Scottish Stone of Destiny—or Stone of Scone—where Scottish kings were traditionally crowned. The original scones were triangle-shaped and were baked on a griddle. Today's scones are round, oval, triangular, square, or diamond-shaped, and they are usually baked in an oven. There are many varieties of scones, including buttermilk, potato, sweet, and oat. Fruit, raisins, molasses, spices, and poppy seeds are also common ingredients.

Looking Back on the United Kingdom

1. Imagine that you decided to start having a traditional English tea every afternoon. Write a plan of how this practice would affect your other daily meals. Would it affect any other parts of your life?

2. Although Scotland, Wales, England, and Northern Ireland are all one nation politically, they each have their own customs and traditions. Use encyclopedias or travel guides to research the culture of one of these four divisions. Write a brief paragraph on what you learn.

3. List the foods of the United Kingdom that you would most like to try. Where can you find these foods? Which can you make?

4. Which foods and food customs of Great Britain are similar to foods and food customs among people where you live? Which are different? How are they different? Create a report to share in class.

Port of Call

Germany

Stretching from the Baltic and North Seas southward to the snowcapped mountains of its southern border, Germany has a little bit of everything! Forests, rivers, hills, plains, valleys, farms, and highly developed industrial cities are some of the sights a visitor can expect to see. In the southern part of Germany, you will come to the Bavarian Alps, the mountain range that includes the country's highest peak. If you travel into the southwestern region, you can wander through the wooded mountains known as the Black Forest. While traveling through this region, be sure to stop for a piece of the famous chocolate-and-cherry Black Forest cake! The middle of Germany, which contains most of its major cities, is made up of low mountains and river valleys. Here you can visit the fertile Rhine Valley, known worldwide for its high-quality grapes. Further north, you will reach the North German Plain—a flat, low region. The eastern end of this plain is one of the best agricultural areas of Germany.

Food Traveler's Notes

Agriculture

German agriculture provides about two-thirds of the food necessary to feed the German population. The best farmland is located in the southern part of the North German Plain. The country's most important crops are wheat, potatoes, sugar beets, and barley. Major fruit crops include apples, grapes, cherries, and strawberries. Pork is Germany's main livestock product and an important part of many German dishes.

People and Language

Approximately 83.5 million people live in Germany. The country is highly industrialized, with many large cities. At least ten German cities have populations of more than half a million people. Most of the larger cities and most industries are located in the western part of Germany.

German is the official language of the country. There are two main forms of this language—High German and Low German. High German, which is the form of German most often used in writing, is spoken mainly in the southern part of the country. People of the North Plain speak Low German. Within the two main categories of High and Low German, there are regional variations or subcategories. Therefore, when traveling through Germany, you may hear several versions of the German language! Two words you are sure to recognize are *pretzel* and *hamburger.* These words and foods originated in the German culture.

Dining

Traditional German cuisine tends to be simple and hearty. Starches and meats have been major parts of the German diet for years, along with cream, eggs, and butter. These heavy traditional foods are still served in parts of Germany, especially rural areas. In recent years, however, many German cooks have begun to "lighten up" their dishes. This move toward lighter cooking is partly because Germans, like people of other cultures, are focusing on making healthy food choices. The new, lighter cuisine of Germany still contains many of the traditional staples, however, such as sauerkraut, pork, and potatoes.

Many German foods have a tangy, sour taste. German cooks use sour cream, vinegar, lemon, and salt to add this flavor to various meat and vegetable dishes. One of Germany's most famous dishes is *sauerbraten,* which actually means "sour roast." This traditional beef roast is marinated in lemon juice and other liquids and covered with spicy, brown, sweet-sour gravy.

(Continued on next page)

German Food Briefs

Wursts

Wurst is the German word for sausage—a favorite of the German people! Germany produces more than 1,500 kinds of wursts, grouped into three categories. *Kochwurst* is the name used for boiled sausages, which include liverwursts and blood or tongue sausages. *Bratwursts* are sausages like frankfurters, which need to be heated before they are eaten. *Hartwursts* or *Rohwursts* are hard, dry, preserved sausages, such as salami and summer sausages, that can be eaten cold. Wursts have become so important in the German culture that when a crucial decision must be made, Germans often say, "The wurst is at stake!"

Sauerkraut (Sour Cabbage)

If you spend enough time in Germany, you are sure to be served a dish containing this salty cabbage! To make sauerkraut, Germans shred cabbage, pack it with salt, press out the juice, and let it ferment. Sauerkraut was actually invented in China during the third century B.C.E. When it was introduced into Europe nearly 1,000 years later, however, it quickly became a German staple. Today, most of the cabbage grown in Germany is made into sauerkraut. Germans sometimes eat it as a side dish, often mixed with apples. More commonly, however, meat and poultry dishes are served over a bed of sauerkraut.

Spaetzle

Spaetzle is the German form of pasta—made of egg batter and shaped in little squiggles or teardrops. Spaetzle are usually served with gravy and are a substitute for potatoes. They can also be layered with cheese in a casserole or baked with sauce and served as a main course.

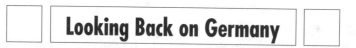

Looking Back on Germany

1. Many German foods have a tangy sour flavor. Can you think of any foods common where you live that also have a sour flavor? What ingredients are used to give them that sour taste? Prepare a list to share in class.

2. Sausages are an important part of the German diet. Use cookbooks to research some recipes for or ways of preparing sausage. Write a brief description of the recipe that sounds best to you.

3. List the foods of Germany that you would most like to try. Where can you find these foods? Which can you make?

4. Imagine you are planning a week's trip to Germany. Use travel guides to research the areas of the country you would most like to see. Make a brief travel plan for your vacation. Which areas of Germany will you visit on which days? What sights do you plan to see?

Cornish Pasties

(Meat and Vegetable Turnovers)

Cornish Pasties
(Meat and Vegetable Turnovers)

Customary	Ingredients	Metric
1 1/2 cups	Diced beef round steak	350 mL
1 cup	Diced potato	250 mL
1/2 cup	Diced onion	125 mL
1/2 cup	Diced carrot	125 mL
1/3 cup	Chopped fresh parsley	75 mL
2 Tbsp.	Water	30 mL
1/2 tsp.	Dill weed	2 mL
1/2 tsp.	Salt	2 mL
1/4 tsp.	Pepper	1 mL
3 cups	All-purpose flour	750 mL
1 1/2 tsp.	Salt	7 mL
1 cup	Shortening	250 mL
1/3 cup	Cold water	75 mL
1 1/2 Tbsp.	Margarine	22 mL
	Milk	

Yield: 15 pasties

Directions

Pan: Baking sheet

1. Preheat oven to 400°F (200°C). Grease baking sheet.

2. Combine beef, potato, onion, carrot, parsley, 2 Tbsp. (30 mL) water, dill weed, 1/2 tsp. (2 mL) salt, and pepper. Cover and refrigerate while preparing pastry.

3. Combine flour and 1 1/2 tsp. (7 mL) salt in medium mixing bowl.

4. Cut shortening into dry ingredients until mixture resembles coarse crumbs.

5. Add cold water, 1 Tbsp. (15 mL) at a time, until dough forms a ball and cleans side of bowl.

6. Divide pastry into thirds. Roll each third into a 12-inch (30-cm) circle. Cut out five 5-inch (13-cm) rounds from each circle.

7. Place 1/4 cup (50 mL) meat mixture on one half of one pastry round. Dot with 1/2 tsp. (2 mL) margarine. Fold over to form a half-circle. Seal edges with a fork, dampening with water if needed. Repeat with remaining pasties.

8. Place pasties on greased baking sheet. Pierce tops with a fork. Brush with milk.

9. Bake at 400°F (200°C) for 10 minutes.

10. Reduce heat to 350°F (180°C). Bake 25 minutes longer.

Nutrition Information: Serving size: 1 pasty

calories: 265	cholesterol: 12 mg	dietary fiber: 1 g
total fat: 17 g	sodium: 318 mg	sugars: 1 g
saturated fat: 4 g	carbohydrate: 21 g	protein: 7 g

Percent Daily Value: vitamin A 16%, vitamin C 4%, calcium 1%, iron 10%

Blaukraut
(German Sweet-Sour Red Cabbage)

Blaukraut
(German Sweet-Sour Red Cabbage)

Customary	Ingredients	Metric
4 slices	Diced bacon	4 slices
6 cups	Shredded red cabbage	1.5 L
1 cup	Apple slices	250 mL
1/2 cup	Thinly sliced onion	125 mL
1/2 cup	Chicken broth	125 mL
2 Tbsp.	Apple cider	30 mL
2 Tbsp.	Vinegar	30 mL
2 Tbsp.	Brown sugar	30 mL
1/2 tsp.	Salt	2 mL
1 tsp.	Caraway seeds (optional)	5 mL

Yield: 4 servings

Conventional Directions

Pan: $2^1/_2$-qt. (2.5-L) saucepan

1. Fry bacon until crisp.

2. Add cabbage, onion, and apple. Cook, uncovered, over medium heat for 5 minutes.

3. Combine broth, apple cider, vinegar, brown sugar, and salt. Stir in cabbage. Sprinkle with caraway seeds, if desired.

4. Cover and cook just until cabbage is tender, 5 to 10 minutes longer.

Microwave Directions

Pan: 3-qt. (3-L) microwave-safe casserole

1. Place bacon between thick layers of white paper towels. Microwave at 100% power for 2 to 3 minutes. Set aside.

2. Combine cabbage, onion, and apple in casserole. Microwave, covered, at 100% power for 7 minutes.

3. Combine broth, apple cider, vinegar, brown sugar, and salt. Stir into cabbage. Sprinkle with caraway seeds, if desired.

4. Microwave, covered, at 100% power for 7 to 8 minutes or until cabbage is tender. Stir in bacon.

Nutrition Information: Serving size: $^1/_4$ recipe

calories: 125
total fat: 4 g
saturated fat: 1 g

cholesterol: 5 mg
sodium: 479 mg
carbohydrate: 20 g

dietary fiber: 3 g
sugars: 14 g
protein: 4 g

Percent Daily Value: vitamin A 6%, vitamin C 108%, calcium 9%, iron 7%

Smorrebrod with Frikadeller

Recipe 21

(Scandinavian Open-Faced Meatball Sandwiches)

Touring Northern Europe

Smorrebrod with Frikadeller
(Scandinavian Open-Faced Meatball Sandwiches)

Customary	Ingredients	Metric
1/2 lb.	Lean ground pork or beef	250 g
2 Tbsp.	All-purpose flour	30 mL
1 Tbsp.	Chopped onion	15 mL
1/2 tsp.	Grated lemon peel	2 mL
1/4 tsp.	Salt	1 mL
1/8 tsp.	Pepper	0.5 mL
1/4 cup	Club soda or water	50 mL
1 Tbsp.	Margarine or butter	15 mL
4 thin slices	Rye bread	4 thin slices
2 tsp.	Softened margarine or butter	10 mL
1/2 cup	Shredded red cabbage	125 mL

Yield: 4 servings

Directions

Pan: Skillet

1. Combine meat, flour, onion, lemon peel, salt, and pepper. Mix thoroughly.

2. Carefully stir in club soda or water.

3. Roll mixture into 12 balls, about 1 1/4 inches (3 cm) in diameter.

4. Heat 1 Tbsp. (15 mL) margarine or butter in skillet. Brown meatballs on all sides.

5. Reduce heat. Simmer, covered, until meatballs are cooked through, about 20 minutes.

6. Refrigerate meatballs until chilled.

7. Spread each slice of bread with 1/2 tsp. (2 mL) softened margarine or butter.

8. Top each piece of bread with a layer of sliced meatballs. Sprinkle with 2 Tbsp. (30 mL) shredded cabbage and serve.

Nutrition Information: Serving size: 1/4 recipe

calories: 256
total fat: 15 g
saturated fat: 5 g
cholesterol: 38 mg
sodium: 404 mg

carbohydrate: 16 g
dietary fiber: 2 g
sugars: 3 g
protein: 13 g

Percent Daily Value: vitamin A 7%, vitamin C 9%, calcium 4%, iron 13%

Touring Eastern Europe and Northern Asia A Global Foods Tour

Map 7 (page 22) shows Poland, the Czech Republic, Slovakia, Hungary, and many of the other countries that make up Eastern Europe. The section of this map labeled Russia and Neighboring Countries is shown in more detail on Map 8 (page 23). To understand how the maps relate to one another, find and mark the Black Sea on both maps. Notice the small European countries of Belarus, the Ukraine, Hungary, and the Baltic states of Estonia, Latvia, and Lithuania. Eastern Europe also includes the countries of the Balkan Peninsula—Greece, Bulgaria, Romania, and others. As you can see on Map 8, Russia, which is the largest country in the world, spills over the border of Europe and sprawls over much of Northern Asia.

The Eastern European and Northern Asian Region make up an enormous area of land containing almost every imaginable geographic feature and a wide range of growing conditions. The European section of Russia, the Ukraine, and much of Poland and Belarus are made up of rolling plains. The Balkan Peninsula is mostly mountainous. Only moss, lichens, and small scrubs grow along Siberia's Arctic Coast, but in the extreme southwest are grasslands, Siberia's richest farming area.

People and Cultures

Most of the people in Eastern Europe and Northern Asia are Slavic people, called Slavs. Approximately 250 million Slavs live in this region. The early Slavic tribes, a group of farmers and herders in eastern Poland and western Russia, eventually expanded throughout Eastern Europe, forming different cultures and languages. Although almost every Eastern European nation today has its own language, most of the languages are similar and are part of the Slavic language group.

Cuisines of Eastern Europe and Northern Asia

Cuisines in this area of the world tend to be rich and filling. Specific foods and cooking styles, however, vary from region to region. Much of today's Slavic cooking is based on foods prepared by the early Slavic peasant farmers. Bread, which was a staple food of the early farmers, is still a very important food in Slavic countries. Foods in the Baltic states are similar to foods of the Scandinavian countries located just across the Baltic Sea. In the regions near Greece, Bulgaria, and the southwestern tip of Russia, foods have a Southwest Asian flavor. Here, lamb, yogurt, chickpeas, and grape leaves are common ingredients.

The Savvy Gourmet

Russia is noted for its caviar, or roe—the salted eggs of one of three kinds of sturgeon fish. Caviar is an expensive treat and is usually eaten alone rather than as an accompaniment to other foods. The color of the jar or tin in which it is sold tells the type of sturgeon it is from. Roe from *beluga* is sold in blue jars or tins, from *sevruga* in red, and from *osetra* in yellow.

Port of Call

Russia

Touring Eastern Europe and Northern Asia

At nearly twice the size of the United States, Russia is the largest country in the world. This enormous nation makes up a large part of Eastern Europe and then stretches even further east to cover the entire northern part of Asia! The dividing line between European Russia and Asian Russia is the Ural Mountain range, which runs north to south across the country.

The European part of Russia is a vast plain, called the European Plain. This is the region that contains almost all of the country's farmland and most of its population. Here, you will find modern cities and small farming villages. You might stop in St. Petersburg for a hearty lunch of three or four courses before you begin your tour of the city's many palaces and cathedrals. As you cross the Ural Mountains and continue traveling east, you will see a very different side of Russia! Here are the harsh, empty stretches of Siberia. Although the western part of Siberia is flat and marshy, its eastern parts are mountainous. If you plan a winter trip to the easternmost point of Siberia, bring your warmest clothing. With temperatures that can drop to -90°F (-68°C), this is the coldest part of Russia!

Food Traveler's Notes

Agriculture

Russia is a major producer of grains—wheat, barley, oats, and rye. Sunflower seeds, sugar beets, potatoes, and certain kinds of vegetables and fruits are also important crops. Most of Russia's farms lie in an area called the "fertile triangle." The base of this triangle runs along Russia's western border between the Baltic Sea and Black Sea. The triangle tip is in southwestern Siberia. Aside from this wedge of fertile land, most of Russia is either too dry or too cold for agriculture.

People and Language

Russia has a total population of more than 148 million people. Most of the people live in European Russia—primarily in the fertile triangle region. Many areas of Russia, where the climate and soil are unfriendly, are nearly empty. More than one-third of the country contains only about three people per square mile (about one per square km). The people of Russia represent more than 100 different nationalities, and each nationality has its own language. Most of the population, however, is Russian, and if you visit Russia, Russian is the language you will hear most.

Dining

To many Russians, breakfast is the most important meal of the day. Through the week, a typical Russian breakfast might include eggs, cold cuts, breads, hot cereal, and tea. On weekends, breakfasts are special family meals. A weekend breakfast menu might include sausage, bacon, sweet cheese patties, and pancakes. The midday meal, usually eaten between noon and 2:00 P.M., is the main meal in Russia. It is typically a large meal, with three to four courses including appetizers, soup, main course, and dessert. Russians eat the final meal of the day, supper, between 6:00 and 8:00 P.M. This is usually the lightest meal of the day, sometimes consisting of just one dish.

(Continued on next page)

Port of Call: Russia (continued)

Russian Food Briefs

Kasha

Foods made from grains are staples of the Russian diet. One of the most common grain dishes is *kasha,* a cooked porridge. In the United States, kasha usually means buckwheat, but in Russia the word is used to refer to any kind of grain porridge—including oatmeal, wheat, barley, and buckwheat. Kasha may be eaten at all three meals and is a very important part of Russian culture and language. In Russia, if someone is all mixed up, he or she is said to have "kasha in the head." To "spoon out the kasha" is to straighten out the confusion.

Borscht

Russia is famous for this hearty, ruby-red beet soup. There are many different recipes for borscht. Some versions contain various combinations of cabbage, carrots, potatoes, onions, garlic, pork, and beef. Borscht is often served chilled in the summer, but in the winter it is usually served piping hot. Most Russians top their bowls of borscht with a dollop of sour cream and perhaps some fresh chopped dill.

Blini

Blini are Russian pancakes, and they are one of the most ancient Slavic dishes. These light, crisp pancakes are often served with sour cream, jam, honey, or butter. Russians also eat blini with cottage cheese, mushrooms, smoked fish, and caviar. Traditionally, blini are part of the Russian spring festival of Maslenitsa. During this festival, which celebrates the death of winter and the beginning of spring, the round blini are used to symbolize the sun.

Looking Back on Russia

1. Russians use the word kasha in a number of folk sayings or phrases. People in the United States also have folk sayings that include food names. For example, the phrase "that takes the cake" is sometimes used to mean "that wins the prize." Can you think of other folk sayings that include food names? List the sayings and their meanings.

2. Use travel guides or an encyclopedia to research a Russian city. Write a brief description of the city, including its location, population, and famous sights or attractions.

3. List the foods of Russia that you would most like to try. Where can you find these foods? Which can you make?

4. In Russia, blini are eaten as part of the spring festival of Maslenitsa. List foods that are commonly eaten as part of holidays in your culture.

Port of Call

Greece

Touring Eastern Europe and Northern Asia

At the tip of the Balkan Peninsula in southeastern Europe is the country of Greece. About four-fifths of Greece, called the mainland, is connected to the continent of Europe. The Greek mainland is bordered on the north by the countries of Albania, Macedonia, Bulgaria, and Turkey. The Aegean Sea lies to Greece's east, and the Ionian Sea lies to its west. To the south is the Mediterranean Sea. About one-fifth of Greece's total land is made up of islands that lie in the Aegean and Ionian seas. Altogether, Greece is approximately the size of the state of Alabama. Use Map 6 (page 21) to locate Greece and then mark its location on Map 7 (page 22).

Greece is known for its natural beauty and its warm, Mediterranean climate. Much of the country is mountainous and rugged. There are, however, several plains on the eastern side of the mainland. The Greek islands are generally mountainous, with dry, stony soil. In the lowland areas of Greece, summers are hot and dry, and winters are rainy—the perfect climate for growing the olives that are such an important part of Greek cuisine!

Food Traveler's Notes

Agriculture

Few crops will grow in the dry, rocky soil of Greece's mountains. Therefore much of the country is unsuitable for farming. In the plain areas, however, the fertile soil and warm climate combine to produce many different kinds of crops. Sugar beets, wheat, corn, olives, and tomatoes are the largest crops. Fruit crops, including grapes, peaches, and citrus fruits, are also common. Poultry, sheep, and goats are the primary kinds of livestock.

People and Language

Approximately 10.6 million people live in the Greek mainland and islands. This is a large number of people for the amount of land available—the overall population density is about 207 persons per square mile (80 per square km.). About 98 percent of the country's total population is Greek. The most common language is Modern Greek, or *Demotike*.

Traditions and family ties are very important to Greeks. Greek holidays are celebrated with traditional foods and food customs. At Easter, the most important Greek holiday, the traditional meal is herb-seasoned, roasted lamb. A braided bread is another traditional Easter food in Greece. Roast pig, holiday breads, and butter cookies are traditional Christmas foods.

Dining

Greek cuisine is based on the foods that grow best in Greece. Olives and olive oils are part of almost every recipe. Many dishes also contain vegetables that are grown locally, such as eggplants, zucchinis, and artichokes. Honey, which is found wild in all parts of Greece, is a sweetener used in many Greek treats.

Greek breakfasts are usually simple and light, often fresh fruit, cheese, bread, and strong coffee. Lunch is usually eaten around 1:00 or 2:00 P.M. In the cities, this meal is also fairly light, much like lunches in the United States. In more rural areas, however, lunch is the main meal of the day. Dinner is a family meal, usually eaten around 10:00 P.M. It may consist of an appetizer, salad, a meat or fish dish, vegetables, and potatoes, pasta, or rice. In areas where lunch is the main meal, however, dinner is usually much lighter.

(Continued on next page)

Greek Food Briefs

Moussaka

The popular Greece dish *moussaka* is served throughout Greece. Traditional moussaka consists of layers of sliced eggplant and ground lamb or beef, baked and covered with a white sauce. Although this eggplant moussaka is most common, variations of the dish contain other kinds of vegetables. For example, a light, summertime version of moussaka uses potatoes and zucchini instead of egg-plant. This version is especially popular in the Greek islands. Another popular version of moussaka is made with artichoke hearts in place of eggplant.

Dolmades

Dolmades (pronounced dohl-mah-dehs) are stuffed grape or cabbage leaves—one of Greece's most famous foods. To make dolmades with grape leaves, the Greek cook either uses leaves fresh off the vine or, more commonly, leaves that have been preserved in salt water. Dolmades may be stuffed with any of a variety of fillings. One of the most popular fillings is a mixture of ground lamb, rice, onion, currants, pine nuts, and various seasonings. Dolmades have a long history in the Greek culture—dating back to ancient Greece, where fig leaves were sometimes used to wrap foods.

Spanakopita

Whether for lunch, dinner, or a snack, *spanikopita*—or spinach pie—is a Greek favorite. The flaky spanikopita crust is made with *phyllo* dough, which is a delicate, tissue-thin pastry. The pie filling is a mixture of spinach, onions, eggs, and feta cheese—a crumbly, salty, white cheese usually made with goat's milk. Spanikopita can either be served hot, as a main dish, or cold, as an appetizer or snack.

Looking Back on Greece

1. Stuffed grape leaves are a very popular Greek dish. List stuffed or rolled foods that are popular where you live. Also include in your list other stuffed or rolled foods that are popular in other cultures.

2. The history of Greece includes nearly four centuries when it was ruled by Turkey. Research and compare several Greek and Turkish recipes. Write a paragraph to summarize your conclusions.

3. List the foods of Greece that you would most like to try. Where can you find these foods? Which can you make?

4. The Greek word *moussaka* refers to a layered vegetable and meat dish, topped with a sauce. Using this information, invent your own moussaka using vegetables and meats that are common where you live. Write down the ingredients for your dish.

Borscht
(Russian Beet Soup)

Borscht
(Russian Beet Soup)

Customary	Ingredients	Metric
2 cups	Peeled, chopped beets	500 mL
1 cup	Thick onion slices	250 mL
1/2 cup	Carrot slices	125 mL
	Water	
2 cups	Beef broth	500 mL
1 cup	Shredded cabbage	250 mL
2 Tbsp.	Vinegar or pickle juice	30 mL
1 Tbsp.	Margarine or butter	15 mL
1 Tbsp.	Sugar	15 mL
1	Bay leaf	1
Dash	Pepper	Dash
4 Tbsp.	Sour cream (optional)	60 mL
	Chopped cucumber (optional)	

Yield: 4 servings

Directions

Pan: 2-qt. (2-L) saucepan

1. Place beets, onion, and carrots in saucepan. Add just enough water to cover. Bring to a boil.

2. Reduce heat. Simmer, covered, about 20 minutes.

3. Stir in broth, cabbage, vinegar or pickle juice, margarine or butter, sugar, bay leaf, and pepper. Simmer, covered, 15 minutes longer.

4. Remove bay leaf. Serve immediately, or chill and serve cold. Top each serving with 1 Tbsp. (15 mL) sour cream and chopped cucumber, if desired.

Nutrition Information: Serving size: About 1 1/4 cup (300 mL)

calories: 99
total fat: 3 g
saturated fat: 1 g
cholesterol: 0 mg
sodium: 476 mg

carbohydrate: 15 g
dietary fiber: 3 g
sugars: 10 g
protein: 3 g

Percent Daily Value: vitamin A 53%, vitamin C 31%, calcium 5%, iron 6%

Tip for Success

◆ Borscht has many variations. If you like, try adding stew meat (beef, pork, or lamb), chopped tomato, dill, garlic, parsley, or lemon juice.

Russian Black Bread

Russian Black Bread

Customary	Ingredients	Metric
1 cup	Water	250 mL
2 Tbsp.	Cider vinegar	30 mL
2 Tbsp.	Molasses	30 mL
1/4 cup	Vegetable oil	50 mL
1 oz.	Unsweetened chocolate	31 g
1/4-oz. pkg.	Active dry yeast	7-g pkg
1/2 tsp.	Sugar	2 mL
1/4 cup	Very warm water, about 110°F (43°C)	50 mL
2 cups	Rye flour	500 mL
1 1/2 cups	All-purpose flour	350 mL
1 cup	100 percent bran cereal	250 mL
1 Tbsp.	Caraway seed	15 mL
1 1/2 tsp.	Salt	7 mL
1 tsp.	Instant coffee granules	5 mL
1 tsp.	Minced onion	5 mL
1/2 tsp.	Fennel seed	2 mL
	Vegetable oil	

Yield: One 8-inch (20-cm) round bread

Directions

Pans: Medium saucepan; 8-inch (20-cm) round cake pan

1. Combine 1 cup (250 mL) water, cider vinegar, molasses, 1/4 cup (50 mL) vegetable oil, and chocolate in saucepan. Bring to a boil. Remove from heat and let cool to lukewarm.

2. Meanwhile, in small bowl, dissolve yeast and sugar in 1/4 cup (50 mL) very warm water. Let stand 10 minutes.

3. In large bowl, combine rye and all-purpose flours; mix well. Reserve 2 cups (500 mL) for later use.

4. To remaining flour mixture, add bran cereal, caraway seed, salt, coffee granules, onion, and fennel seed.

5. Stir in lukewarm, chocolate mixture into flour mixture.

6. Add yeast mixture. Beat until smooth.

7. Stir in enough of reserved flour mixture to make a soft dough.

(Continued on next page)

Recipe 23 Russian Black Bread (continued)

8. Shape dough into a ball. Place in a greased bowl, turning to coat all sides. Cover dough with plastic wrap; cover bowl with a clean dish towel. Let rise in a warm place for about 1 hour.

9. Punch dough down. Knead in remaining flour mixture until dough is smooth.

10. Grease 8-inch (20-cm) round baking pan. Press dough into pan. Brush top lightly with vegetable oil.

11. Cover and let rise in a warm place until double, about 1^1/$_2$ hours.

12. Preheat oven to 350°F (180°C). Bake loaf for about 50 minutes, or until bread sounds hollow when tapped. Remove from pan and let cool on wire rack.

Nutrition Information: Serving size: 1 slice (32 per loaf)

calories: 73
total fat: 2 g
saturated fat: 0 g
cholesterol: 0 mg
sodium: 115 mg

carbohydrate: 12 g
dietary fiber: 1 g
sugars: 2 g
protein: 2 g

Percent Daily Value: vitamin A 0%, vitamin C 3%, calcium 1%, iron 5%

Kasha

Kasha

Customary	Ingredients	Metric
1 cup	Kasha (buckwheat groats)	250 mL
1	Egg, beaten	1
2 cups	Chicken broth	500 mL
2 Tbsp.	Margarine	30 mL
1/2 tsp.	Salt	2 mL
1/4 tsp.	Pepper	1 mL

Yield: 4 servings

Directions

Pans: Skillet; 1-qt. (1-L) saucepan

1. Toast kasha in skillet over low heat, stirring frequently.

2. Quickly stir in egg. Cook, stirring and chopping mixture, until egg is cooked and kernels have separated, about 3 minutes.

3. Combine broth, margarine, salt, and pepper in saucepan. Bring to a boil.

4. Stir broth mixture into kasha. Simmer, covered, until kernels are fluffy and tender, about 15 minutes.

5. Fluff with fork and serve.

Nutrition Information: Serving size: 3/4 cup (175 mL)

calories: 231
total fat: 9 g
saturated fat: 2 g
cholesterol: 53 mg
sodium: 741 mg

carbohydrate: 32 g
dietary fiber: 3 g
sugars: 0 g
protein: 9 g

Percent Daily Value: vitamin A 11%, vitamin C 0%, calcium 2%, iron 9%

Avgolemono
(Greek Egg-Lemon Soup)

Avgolemono
(Greek Egg-Lemon Soup)

Customary	Ingredients	Metric
6 cups	Chicken broth	1.5 L
1/3 cup	Long-grain rice	75 mL
2	Eggs	2
1/4 cup	Lemon juice	50 mL
	Salt (to taste)	
	White pepper (to taste)	

Yield: 4 servings

Directions

Pan: 2-qt. (2-L) saucepan

1. Combine broth and rice in saucepan. Bring to a boil.

2. Reduce heat. Simmer until rice is cooked, about 15 minutes.

3. Beat eggs. Gradually add lemon juice, stirring constantly.

4. Gradually add 1/4 cup (50 mL) hot broth to egg mixture, stirring constantly.

5. Gradually pour egg mixture into saucepan, stirring constantly.

6. Reduce heat. Cook until soup is heated through, about 3 minutes.

7. Season to taste with salt and white pepper. Serve hot.

Nutrition Information: Serving size: 1/4 recipe

calories: 156
total fat: 5 g
saturated fat: 1 g
cholesterol: 107 mg
sodium: 1196 mg

carbohydrate: 15 g
dietary fiber: 0 g
sugars: 0.3 g
protein: 12 g

Percent Daily Value: vitamin A 5%, vitamin C 11%, calcium 3%, iron 11%

Tip for Success

◆ The gradual blending of ingredients, with constant stirring, helps keep the egg from curdling.

Goulash
(Hungarian Stew)

Recipe 26

Touring Eastern Europe and Northern Asia

Goulash
(Hungarian Stew)

Customary	Ingredients	Metric
2 Tbsp.	Vegetable oil	30 mL
1 lb.	Stew meat (beef, veal, pork, or lamb) cut in 1-inch (2.5-cm) cubes	500 g
1 cup	Chopped onion	250 mL
1 cup	Diced green pepper	250 mL
1 cup	Chicken broth or tomato juice	250 mL
1 Tbsp.	Hungarian sweet paprika	15 mL
1/2 tsp.	Salt	2 mL
4 small	Potatoes, peeled and diced	4 small
	Hot cooked noodles	

Yield: 4 servings

Directions

Pan: 2-qt. (2-L) heavy saucepan

1. Heat oil in saucepan. Add meat and brown on all sides.

2. Add onion and green pepper. Sauté for about 3 minutes.

3. Stir in broth or juice, paprika, and salt. Bring to a boil.

4. Reduce heat. Simmer, covered, about 1 hour.

5. Add potatoes. Continue to simmer, covered, for 30 minutes longer.

6. Serve over noodles.

Nutrition Information: Serving size: 1/4 recipe (using beef; without noodles)

calories: 513
total fat: 31 g
saturated fat: 10 g
cholesterol: 79 mg
sodium: 519 mg

carbohydrate: 33 g
dietary fiber: 3 g
sugars: 4 g
protein: 26 g

Percent Daily Value: vitamin A 13%, vitamin C 62%, calcium 3%, iron 22%

Dobos Torta

(Hungarian Torte)

**Dobos Torta
(Hungarian Torte)**

Customary	Ingredients	Metric
	Chocolate Cream Filling:	
1/4 cup	Cornstarch	50 mL
1/4 cup	Sugar	50 mL
11/4 cup	Skim milk	300 mL
1	Egg yolk, beaten	1
1 cup	Butter or margarine	250 mL
1 cup	Marshmallows	250 mL
2 oz.	Semisweet chocolate	62 g
	Cake Batter:	
6	Eggs, separated	6
3/4 cup	Sugar, divided	175 mL
1 cup	Flour	250 mL
1 tsp.	Baking powder	5 mL
1/4 tsp.	Salt	1 mL
	Caramel Glaze:	
1 Tbsp.	Butter or margarine	15 mL
1 cup	Sugar	250 mL

Yield: 12 servings

Directions

Pans: 1-qt. (1-L) saucepan; double boiler; baking sheets

1. Mix cornstarch and 1/4 cup (50 mL) sugar in saucepan. Gradually add milk. Stir until smooth.

2. Cook mixture over low heat, stirring constantly, until thick, about 5 to 10 minutes.

3. Gradually add a few tablespoons milk mixture to 1 beaten egg yolk, stirring constantly.

4. Pour egg mixture into saucepan, stirring constantly until well blended. Transfer mixture into a heat-resistant bowl. Let cool.

5. Cream 1 cup (250 mL) butter or margarine until light and fluffy. Gradually beat into cooled milk mixture.

6. Melt marshmallows and chocolate in a double boiler over low heat (or in a microwave oven), stirring frequently until smooth.

(Continued on next page)

Recipe 27 Dobos Torta (continued)

7. Beat chocolate mixture into milk mixture.

8. Cover and refrigerate filling while preparing cake.

9. Preheat oven to 425°F (220°C). Grease and flour baking sheets.

10. In large bowl, beat 6 egg yolks with $1/2$ cup (125 mL) sugar until thick and pale, about 5 minutes. Set aside.

11. In a separate, clean bowl, beat 6 egg whites until foamy. Gradually beat in $1/4$ cup (50 mL) sugar until stiff peaks form.

12. Fold egg white mixture into egg yolk mixture.

13. Combine flour, baking powder, and salt.

14. Sift flour mixture over egg mixture. Gently fold dry ingredients into batter.

15. Spread batter in six 10-inch (25-cm) rounds on prepared baking sheets.

16. Bake at 425°F (220°C) for 5 to 7 minutes, or until toothpick inserted in center comes out clean.

17. Remove cake layers from sheets and cool on wire racks.

18. Spread chocolate cream filling on five of the cake layers.

19. Place one frosted cake layer on serving plate. Top with remaining frosted layers. Place unfrosted layer on top.

20. Combine 1 Tbsp. (15 mL) butter or margarine and 1 cup (250 mL) sugar in a heavy saucepan.

21. Cook over low heat, stirring slowly and constantly, until sugar has dissolved and mixture is light brown and bubbly.

22. Immediately spread caramel glaze over top of torte. While glaze is still warm, use an oiled knife to score it into 12 equal wedges.

23. Chill torte several hours or overnight.

Nutrition Information: Serving size: $1/12$ recipe

calories: 401
total fat: 21 g
saturated fat: 4 g
cholesterol: 125 mg
sodium: 307 mg

carbohydrate: 51 g
dietary fiber: 0 g
sugars: 37 g
protein: 6 g

Percent Daily Value: vitamin A 33%, vitamin C 0%, calcium 7%, iron 7%

Touring East and Southeast Asia A Global Foods Tour

Find the countries of East and Southeast Asia on Map 9 (page 24). These countries stretch from the southeastern border of Russia southward and eastward into the Indian and Pacific Oceans. The largest part of this region is the country of China. All of the other East and Southeast Asian nations could fit inside China and still have room to spare! Along with China, several smaller nations make up the East and Southeast Asian mainland, including Mongolia, Burma, Thailand, Vietnam, and North and South Korea. The island nations of Japan, Indonesia, Taiwan, and the Philippines make up the rest of the region.

There is a wide range of temperatures and weathers in the East and Southeast Asian countries. In the northern reaches of Mongolia, China, and Japan, the winds from Siberia blow in cold, dry winters. Southeastern China and the countries further south have subtropical to tropical climates with hot, humid summers and very mild winters. Indonesia and the Philippines are very near the equator, so they are generally hot and damp year-round.

People and Cultures

The southeast quarter of Asia is the most heavily populated part of the entire Asian continent. Overcrowding is common in this region, with more than 1,500 people often living in a square mile of land (3,900 people per square km). Some of the East and Southeast Asian countries are very rural, while others are highly urbanized. In Laos and Thailand, for example, more than three-quarters of the people live in small, rural settlements. In Japan, Taiwan, and South Korea, however, most of the people live in cities.

Cuisines of East and Southeast Asia

Harmony and balance are key concepts in the cuisines of East and Southeast Asia. In these cultures, it is important that meals have a good balance of textures, temperatures, and flavors. Most of the dishes of this region feature foods that are fresh and locally raised. Therefore rice and seafood are menu staples in almost every East and Southeast Asian country. In Southeast Asia, meals are often fiery hot, flavored with spices grown in the famous Spice Islands of Indonesia. Coconut is also an important ingredient in foods of this area. Southeast Asian cooks commonly use coconut milk instead of cow's milk.

The Savvy Gourmet

When dining in East and Southeast Asia, watch for pickles! They are used to add flavor to many dishes, but don't expect just the usual cucumber varieties common in the United States. In Asia, pickles might be made from any food including cabbage, ginseng, and pumpkins.

Port of Call

Japan

Touring East and Southeast Asia

Off the eastern coast of Asia lies the island nation of Japan. Japan consists of four large, main islands and more than 1,000 smaller ones. Of the four large islands, Honshu is the largest, Skikoku is the smallest, Hokkaido is the furthest north, and Kyushu is the furthest south. Altogether, Japan is slightly smaller than the state of California. Most of it is rugged, with high mountains, deep valleys, and winding coastlines. The main mountains run north to south, with smaller ranges branching out east and west toward the coasts.

Japan's climate varies widely from the north end to the south end. Hokkaido, the northern island, has short summers and long severe winters. The islands further south are much warmer, with hot, humid summers and mild winters.

Food Traveler's Notes

Agriculture

Land is scarce in Japan, and most of the land that is available is not good farmland. Japanese farmers grow more rice than any other crop—more than 40 percent of all farmland is used for rice. Not surprisingly, rice plays a major role in the Japanese diet. Other crops include sugar beets, potatoes, cabbage, and citrus fruits, and sugarcane. Seafood is almost as important as rice in Japanese cuisine. The Japanese fishing fleet is one of the largest in the world, and fishing is a major industry in these islands.

People and Language

Japan is one of the most crowded countries in the world. To get a sense of how crowded it is, consider that the state of California has only around 30 million inhabitants. Japan, which covers a slightly smaller area, is home to more than 125.5 million people.

Japan is highly industrialized and has many cities. Almost half of the people live in the major cities of Tokyo, Osaka, and Nagoya. Japanese is the official language of the country. However, many Japanese people also know some English, because it is taught in most secondary schools and is often used in business dealings.

Most Japanese people practice religions called Shinto and Buddhism. Both religions stress the importance of honor, courage, politeness, self-control, and harmony with nature. Japanese etiquette is guided by these important principles.

Dining

To the Japanese, a food's appearance is just as important as its taste. Japanese chefs have made an art form of slicing foods into precise shapes and arranging them artistically. Meals are prepared and presented to achieve a balance of colors, textures, tastes, and shapes. Even the serving dishes are important in Japanese cuisine! Cooks select dishware to harmonize with the meal and the season. Most foods are simple, fresh, and locally grown. Many foods are served raw or only slightly cooked to preserve and highlight their freshness.

Most meals are fairly light, with smaller portions than are common in western cultures. Rice and soup are served at all three meals. Small pickled items, such as vegetables and tiny whole fish, are also part of every meal. Desserts consist of fruit or a variety of cakes or buns. The Japanese eat with chopsticks and drink their soup directly from the bowl.

(Continued on next page)

Port of Call: Japan (continued)

Japanese Food Briefs

Sushi

When Americans think of Japanese cuisine, sushi is often the first thing that comes to mind. This well-known specialty contains boiled rice, flavored with a sweetened rice vinegar. The Japanese add different ingredients to the rice and form it into different shapes to make a variety of sushi types. Common sushi ingredients include raw fish, tofu, mushrooms, and various fresh and pickled vegetables. Sushi is often rolled into *nori,* thin sheets of seaweed. In Japan, sushi is a finger food and can be served as appetizers, snacks, or a full meal. It is usually served with a soy sauce for dipping and sometimes with strips of pickled ginger.

Sashimi

Sashimi is the Japanese name for any type of raw fish eaten alone. Several kinds of fish are used for sashimi, including sea bass, red snapper, squid, abalone, and the Japanese favorite, tunny fish. The most important aspect of sashimi is its freshness. Ideally, the fish should be no more than 12 hours old and well refrigerated, but never frozen. The second most important aspect of sashimi is the way it is sliced. There are four basic ways to cut the fish, and expert sashimi chefs know which cuts to use with each kind of fish. Sashimi is served with soy sauce and *wasabi,* a strong green horseradish for dipping.

Tempura

Not all seafood in Japan is eaten raw! In *tempura,* fresh pieces of seafood and vegetables are dipped in batter and deep-fried to a golden brown. Common seafoods used to make tempura are prawns, squid, shrimp, scallops, and other kinds of fish. Vegetables include eggplant, green pepper, sweet potato, mushrooms, onion, and carrot. Most tempura meals contain at least six different kinds of food, chosen not only for their tastes but also for their color, shape, and texture. They are served with a variety of sauces.

Looking Back on Japan

1. Rice is served at almost every Japanese meal. What, if any, food items are served at most of the meals in your culture? Brainstorm and list as many as you can. Discuss in class.

2. Much of the Japanese people's behavior—from cooking to arranging furniture to planting gardens—is influenced by the concepts of harmony and balance. Do you think these concepts influence the behavior of people in your culture? Why or why not? Write a brief report answering these questions.

3. List the foods of Japan that you would most like to try. Where can you find these foods? Which can you make?

4. Do you think that Japanese foods are generally more or less healthful for people to eat than those eaten in the western culture? Explain your answer.

Port of Call

Vietnam

The S-shaped country of Vietnam is sometimes described as a long bamboo pole with a rice basket hanging from each end. The top "rice basket" is the widest part of Vietnam, bordered on the north by China. This area contains the Red River Delta, a flat, fertile triangle of land. The bottom "rice basket" is the Mekong River Delta, another fertile lowland. Between these two deltas is a long, skinny stretch of high, coastal land. Vietnam is bordered on the west by the countries of Laos and Cambodia, and on the east and south by the South China Sea.

Because it is not far north of the equator, Vietnam has warm temperatures year-round. The northern parts of the country are subtropical, with dry winters and wet summers. Central and southeastern areas of Vietnam are tropical, with high temperatures and lots of rain.

Food Traveler's Notes

Agriculture

Agriculture is the biggest part of the Vietnamese economy. The country is the world's third-largest exporter of rice—which is its main crop. Other important crops include sugarcane, sweet potatoes, and cassava, which is a tropical plant with edible roots. Fishing is also a very important source of food for the Vietnamese people. Vietnam's long coastline and many streams provide an excellent supply of fish and other seafood.

People and Language

Most of the 73.9 million people of Vietnam live in small villages in the delta areas or along the coast. The southern delta area has most of Vietnam's larger cities. About 88 percent of all the country's people are Vietnamese and speak the Vietnamese language.

During parts of its history, Vietnam has been conquered and ruled by both the Chinese and the French. Elements of Chinese and French culture can still be seen in Vietnamese culture and cuisine today. For example, the Vietnamese adopted the use of chopsticks and the practice of stir-frying from the Chinese. From the French came two current day Vietnamese favorites—crusty loaves of white bread and a ground pork paste called a *pâté*.

Dining

Traveling from north to south in Vietnam, a visitor can expect to find different regional foods and flavors. In north Vietnam, near the border with China, foods reflect a Chinese influence. Stir-fried dishes, soups, and a soupy rice porridge called *chao* are very popular. Dishes in this region are less spicy than those eaten in other parts of the country. In the hot, humid south of Vietnam, the cuisine features many of the foods that grow locally. Coconut milk, pineapple, sugarcane, tomatoes, and bean sprouts are favorite ingredients. Southern Vietnamese foods tend to be sweeter, spicier, and heartier than those in the northern and central regions. Despite regional differences, however, visitors to any part of Vietnam can expect to find rice and seafood at practically every meal.

A typical Vietnamese meal includes soup, a stir-fry, another main dish, and often a light salad. The food is all served at once and shared from common serving dishes. When someone's bowl is empty, the serving dishes are passed around again—second and third helpings are common in this culture!

(Continued on next page)

Vietnamese Food Briefs

Pho

The Vietnamese word for noodle soup is *pho,* which translates to "your own bowl." This means that each person's food is in his or her own bowl, instead of in a common serving bowl. Noodle soups are a favorite breakfast food in Vietnam, and people also eat these hearty soups all through-out the day. Soup vendors are very common in Vietnam. One of the most popular soups in northern Vietnam is *pho bo,* a beef and noodle soup seasoned with cinnamon, cloves, ginger, and other spices. Pho bo, like many other soups, is served with a variety of toppings, including lime wedges, bean sprouts, chilies, and chopped onion.

Nuoc Mam

Nuoc mam is a reddish fish sauce made of fermented anchovies. This salty fish sauce is a crucial ingredient in most Vietnamese dishes. In many dishes, it is used in the place of salt. Vietnamese cooks frequently mix nuoc mam with lime juice, chilies, garlic, vinegar, and sugar to make a hot sauce called *nuoc cham.* Nuoc cham is served at practically every Vietnamese meal and is used as a salad dressing and a dipping sauce.

Desserts

The Vietnamese typically end their meals with a variety of fruits common to the area. Apples, oranges, bananas, and starfruit are common desserts, as well as more exotic tropical fruits like bright red Malaysian *rambutans* or yellow plum-like *loquats.* On special occasions, Vietnamese cooks might serve a dessert other than fruit. Treats made with coconut, such as a coconut custard called *flan,* coconut rice cakes, or cookies, are the most common desserts.

Looking Back on Vietnam

1. The Vietnamese have adopted certain foods and ways of eating from China and France. In the cuisine of your culture, are there certain foods that have been adopted from other cultures? List the foods and the cultures they come from.

2. Use travel guides or an encyclopedia to research a city in Vietnam that interests you. Write a brief description of the city, including information on its location and size. List the sights of the city you would most like to see.

3. List the foods of Vietnam that you would most like to try. Where can you find these foods? Which can you make?

4. The fish sauce *nuoc mam* is used to flavor almost all Vietnamese dishes. In the cuisine of your cultures, is there a flavor or flavors that are used to season many dishes? Brainstorm ideas with your classmates.

Maki-Sushi

(Rolled Vinegar Rice of Japan)

Recipe 28

Touring East and Southeast Asia

Maki-Sushi
(Rolled Vinegar Rice of Japan)

Customary	Ingredients	Metric
2 sheets	Nori (seaweed)	2 sheets
1/2 cup	Short-grained rice	125 mL
1/2 cup	Water	125 mL
1 small piece	Konbu (dried kelp)	1 small piece
3 Tbsp.	Rice vinegar	45 mL
1 Tbsp.	Sugar	15 mL
1/2 tsp.	Salt	2 mL
1	Cucumber	1

Yield: 12 appetizers or snacks

Directions

Pans: 1-qt. (1-L) saucepan; small saucepan

1. Toast nori by passing the shiny side over low heat until crispy, 1 to 2 seconds. Set aside.

2. Rinse and drain rice. Place in 1-qt. (1-L) saucepan. Add enough water to cover. Let stand 30 minutes.

3. Drain rice. Add 1/2 cup (125 mL) water and konbu. Bring to a boil.

4. Boil 2 minutes. Remove and discard konbu.

5. Reduce heat. Simmer rice, covered, 15 minutes.

6. Remove rice from heat. Let stand, covered, 10 minutes.

7. Meanwhile, heat vinegar in small saucepan with sugar and salt just until sugar and salt dissolve. Set aside to cool.

8. Cut two long sticks from the cucumber, about 1/2 inch (1.25 cm) on each side and as long as the sheets of nori. Set aside. (Refrigerate remaining cucumber for another use.)

9. Transfer rice to a heat-resistant bowl. Stir in vinegar mixture, fanning rice so it does not get soggy. Continue stirring and fanning for about 2 minutes longer.

10. Spread about 3/4 cup (175 mL) rice mixture on one sheet of nori. Leave a space of about 1/2 inch (1.25 cm) on each of the long sides.

11. Place a cucumber stick lengthwise down the center of the rice.

12. Carefully roll nori from the long side, jelly roll fashion.

(Continued on next page)

Recipe 28 Maki-Sushi (continued)

13. Repeat steps 10-12 with other sheet of nori.

14. Slice each roll into 6 pieces.

15. Arrange sushi attractively on a plate and serve.

Nutrition Information: Serving size: 1 piece maki-sushi

calories: 32
total fat: 0 g
saturated fat: 0 g
cholesterol: 0 mg
sodium: 129 mg

carbohydrate: 7 g
dietary fiber: 2 g
sugars: 1 g
protein: 2 g

Percent Daily Value: vitamin A 15%, vitamin C 17%, calcium 5%, iron 6%

Tip for Success

◆ Maki-Sushi is traditionally formed using a bamboo mat called a *sudare*. The nori is filled on top of the sudare, which is then used as a guide between the hand and the nori as the maki-sushi is rolled.

Steamed Ginger Chicken

(Vietnamese Main Dish)

Recipe 29

Touring East and Southeast Asia

Steamed Ginger Chicken
(Vietnamese Main Dish)

Customary	Ingredients	Metric
1 lb.	Boneless, skinless chicken breast meat	500 g
1/2 cup	Sliced mushrooms	125 mL
1/2 cup	Chopped tomato	125 mL
1	Chopped green onion	1
1 tsp.	Nuoc-mam (Vietnamese fish sauce)	5 mL
1 tsp.	Vegetable oil	5 mL
1 tsp.	Grated fresh ginger	5 mL
1/2 tsp.	Sugar	2 mL
1/8 tsp.	Salt	0.5 mL
1/8 tsp.	Pepper	0.5 mL
	Hot, cooked rice	

Yield: 4 servings

Directions

Pan: Large saucepan; deep, heatproof bowl that fits in saucepan

1. Cut chicken into 1-inch (2.5-cm) chunks.

2. Toss chicken with mushrooms, tomato, and onion in deep, heatproof bowl.

3. Add nuoc-mam, vegetable oil, ginger, sugar, salt, and pepper. Mix well.

4. Add water to saucepan to a depth of 1 inch (2.5 cm). Place bowl with chicken mixture inside saucepan. Cover saucepan, leaving a small opening for steam to escape.

5. Bring water to a boil. Steam over medium heat until chicken is thoroughly cooked, about 30 minutes. Add boiling water to saucepan as needed to replace water lost through evaporation.

6. Serve over hot, cooked rice.

Nutrition Information: Serving size: 1/4 recipe (without rice)

calories: 211
total fat: 5 g
saturated fat: 1 g
cholesterol: 96 mg
sodium: 281 mg

carbohydrate: 3 g
dietary fiber: 0 g
sugars: 1 g
protein: 36 g

Percent Daily Value: vitamin A 3%, vitamin C 9%, calcium 3%, iron 10%

Chinese Bean Sprout Salad

Recipe 30

Touring East and Southeast Asia

Chinese Bean Sprout Salad

Customary	Ingredients	Metric
1/4 cup	Pine nuts or sliced almonds	50 mL
2 cups	Mung bean sprouts	500 mL
1 cup	Shredded carrots	250 mL
1/2 cup	Diced red bell pepper	125 mL
2	Chopped green onion	2
1/3 cup	Rice vinegar	75 mL
1/4 cup	Sesame or peanut oil	50 mL
2 Tbsp.	Soy sauce	30 mL
1/4 tsp.	Pepper	1 mL

Yield: 4 servings

Directions

Pan: Shallow baking pan

1. Place nuts in shallow baking pan. Toast in oven at 250°F (120°C) for 15 minutes, stirring every 5 minutes. Cool.

2. Combine nuts, bean sprouts, carrot, red pepper, and green onion in large bowl. If preparing ahead of time, refrigerate until serving.

3. Just before serving, blend vinegar, oil, soy sauce, and pepper. Pour over vegetable and toss to coat.

Nutrition Information: Serving size: 1/4 recipe

calories: 208
total fat: 18 g
saturated fat: 2 g
cholesterol: 0 mg
sodium: 528 mg

carbohydrate: 11 g
dietary fiber: 3 g
sugars: 5 g
protein: 4 g

Percent Daily Value: vitamin A 99%, vitamin C 45%, calcium 5%, iron 8%

Kimchi
(Spicy Korean Relish)

Kimchi
(Spicy Korean Relish)

Customary	Ingredients	Metric
1 head	Napa cabbage, cut into shreds	1 head
2	Green onions, minced	2
1 small	Carrot, shredded	1 small
1 small	Daikon radish, sliced	1 small
3 Tbsp.	Coarse or kosher salt	45 mL
3 cups	Water	750 mL
2 Tbsp.	Korean red pepper flakes	30 mL
2 tsp.	Garlic, minced	10 mL
1 tsp.	Grated fresh ginger	5 mL
1 tsp.	Paprika	5 mL
1/2 tsp.	Sugar	2 mL

Yield: About 4 cups relish

Directions

1. Combine cabbage, onion, carrot, radish, and salt in a large glass bowl.

2. Add water. Cover mixture with a plate and weight down with a heavy object. Let stand 4 hours.

3. Combine red pepper flakes, garlic, ginger, paprika, and sugar.

4. Drain vegetable mixture. Stir spice mixture into vegetable mixture.

5. Place kimchi in a covered, non-plastic container. Refrigerate 1 week to let mixture cure.

6. Serve as a condiment.

Nutrition Information: Serving size: 1/4 cup (50 mL)

calories: 11
total fat: 0 g
saturated fat: 0 g
cholesterol: 0 mg
sodium: 1206 mg

carbohydrate: 2 g
dietary fiber: 1 g
sugars: 1 g
protein: 0 g

Percent Daily Value: vitamin A 21%, vitamin C 20%, calcium 2%, iron 1%

Tip for Success

◆ Korean red pepper flakes are not as hot as regular red pepper flakes. If the Korean variety is not available, substitute a smaller amount of regular red pepper flakes or a dash of hot pepper sauce.

Touring South Asia

A Global Foods Tour

If you look at Map 9 (page 24) you will see that the largest part of South Asia is the Indian Peninsula, a fat triangle of land extending south into the Indian Ocean. At the widest part of the triangle, an arm of India stretches east to the country of Myanmar (formerly Burma). Three smaller nations—Nepal, Bhutan, and Bangladesh—are nestled into this arm. The Himalayan Mountains lie to the north, making a natural border between the South Asian countries and China. At India's northwest edge lies the country of Pakistan, and off the southeastern tip of the Indian Peninsula is the small island nation of Sri Lanka.

People and Cultures

More than 1.2 billion people live in the South Asian countries. Most people of the region live in India. However, Bangladesh, which is not quite as large as the state of Wisconsin, is home to more than 125 million people. This means Bangladesh has the highest population density of any country in the world—more than 1,976 people per square mile (763 per square km). In general South Asia is a rural region, and most people live in small villages.

Most South Asians follow one of two major religions—Hinduism and Islam. Both Hinduism and Islam are ancient religions that involve a whole way of life. Followers of these religions live by strict rules that govern clothing, marriage, family life, and food choices.

Cuisines of South Asia

South Asian cuisines are greatly affected by the dietary laws of Hinduism and Islam. For example, Islamic peoples are not allowed to eat pork, but they can eat beef and other kinds of meat. Hindus, on the other hand, never eat beef, because they consider the cow to be sacred. Climate and geography also influence South Asian cuisine. Rice, which grows well in the region, is a staple food in most South Asian diets. Along the coastal areas of the region, seafood is also a common menu item. South Asian cuisine is perhaps best known for its many spices. Almost every South Asian kitchen contains a wide array of spices—including curry, cumin, coriander, turmeric, cinnamon, ginger, and cloves.

The Savvy Gourmet

You may be surprised at the taste of some familiar spices in South Asia. Most South Asian cooks do not use the already-ground spices common in western kitchens. Instead, they buy their spices whole and grind them by hand in small amounts. The spice flavors are sure to be fresh and, sometimes, powerful!

Port of Call

India

Stretching south from the Asian mainland into the Indian Ocean is the country of India. India is approximately one-third the size of the United States. India is a land of geographic contrasts. At its northeast edge lie the Himalayas, the highest mountains in the world. Just south of the Himalayas is a large stretch of plains, watered by three major Indian rivers. Because of the plentiful supply of water and the rich soil, this region is the most fertile area of the country.

Except for the high Himalayas, India has a tropical climate. Its seasons are determined by the monsoons—seasonal winds that blow from the southwest in summer and the northeast in winter. Between June and October is the season the southwestern monsoon. This wet wind blows in from the Arabian Sea, bringing with it large amounts of rain. From December to February, the northeastern monsoon blows in, bringing cooler, dry weather.

Food Traveler's Notes

Agriculture

Rice and wheat are important crops in India. Most of the nation's wheat is grown in the northern plains, while the southern areas produce most of the rice. Both of these foods are extremely important in Indian cuisine. Other common crops include sugarcane, corn, barley, chickpeas, bananas, and mangoes. India is also known for its many spice crops.

People and Language

India's cultures are so varied that it is difficult to classify the many tribes, races, and cultures that make up this large population. In language, too, the Indian people are diverse, with more than 1,000 different languages spoken in different regions. One thing that many Indians do have in common, however, is their religion. About 83 percent of all Indians are Hindus. Eleven percent are Muslims—followers of Islam.

The dietary laws of these two religions have an enormous influence on Indian foods. Muslims do not eat any pork or pork products, while Hindus do not eat beef. Many Hindus, in fact, eat no meat products at all, even avoiding seafood and eggs. Therefore, Indian cuisines depend heavily on vegetables. To supply the necessary protein that they don't get from meat, Indians use many *pulses* in their cooking. Pulses are dried seeds of legumes, including peas, beans, and lentils.

Dining

Because there is such a variety of people and cultures in India, there is no one pattern for daily meals. A typical Indian meal consists of one main dish—either a vegetable, poultry, fish, or meat combination—rice or bread, and one or two spicy vegetable side dishes. Although they may be served on special occasions, desserts are not usually included in daily meals.

Indian people usually sit on the floor to eat, using trays containing small, individual dishes of the various foods. Traditionally, Indians do not use forks and spoons. They eat with their hands, using pieces of bread to scoop up foods with sauces.

(Continued on next page)

Indian Food Briefs

Mulligatawny Soup

This spicy chicken soup was invented more than 200 years ago in Madras, a city in southeastern India. Its unusual name means "pepper water" in Tamil, the language spoken in that region. The base for mulligatawny is chicken broth, potatoes, lentils, and other vegetables, depending upon the recipe. Once the base is made, the all-important seasonings are added! Although there are many variations of mulligatawny, they all include lots of spices. One super-spicy recipe calls for nine different spices—garlic, chili pepper, cinnamon, cloves, ginger, coriander, cumin, turmeric, and curry! Some versions of mulligatawny also include apples and coconut milk.

Raita

Indians often cool off their spicy-hot meals by including a *raita* on the menu. A raita is a sort of salad, consisting of thick, whole-milk yogurt mixed with various chopped vegetables, fruits, and seasonings. Cucumbers, eggplant, potatoes, spinach, tomatoes, and bananas are some common raita ingredients. Seasonings often include dill, mint, coriander, parsley, and pepper. Many Indian cooks make their own yogurt for this dish—often out of milk from water buffalo!

Tandoori Foods

The Indian word *tandoor* refers to a traditional brick and clay oven with a rounded top. In a tandoor, foods are baked over direct heat produced by a charcoal-fueled fire. The heat in these ovens is intense—usually over 500°F (260°C)! Foods that are baked this way are often identified by the word *tandoori.* For example, Indians eat tandoori lobster, tandoori chicken, and tandoori shrimp—all baked in a tandoor. A favorite Indian bread called *naan* is also made in a tandoor. To make naan, the cook puts bread dough directly onto the oven's clay walls and lets it bake until it is puffy and browned.

Looking Back on India

1. Much Indian cooking is vegetarian, often using pulses as a meat substitute to supply protein. Research and write a report about meat substitutes in vegetarian dishes people in your area use. What other foods are used in these dishes?

2. List which customs and foods of India are most different from the customs and foods you are accustomed to. In a second column, list which ones are the most familiar to you.

3. List the foods of India that you would most like to try. Where can you find these foods? Which can you make?

4. Religious laws limit the kinds of foods many Indian people can eat. Are there any religious laws concerning food that are followed by people in your community? Which foods do they limit?

Port of Call
Sri Lanka

Less than 40 miles (64 km) from the southeastern tip of India lies the teardrop-shaped island of Sri Lanka. In the Sri Lankan language, the name of the island means "resplendent land." Sri Lanka is also sometimes called "the pearl of the Indian Ocean" because of its shape and its great natural beauty. The island, which is home to almost 19 million people, is slightly larger than the state of West Virginia.

Although there are mountains in the south central part of Sri Lanka, most of the island consists of flat or gently rolling plains. Because the island is so near the equator, its climate is typically hot and humid. During the summer months, the monsoon blows in heavy rainfall, especially in the south-western region of the island.

Food Traveler's Notes

Agriculture

Like most nations in the southern and eastern parts of Asia, Sri Lanka's main crop is rice. More Sri Lankan land is devoted to rice than to any other kind of crop. Farmers here also grow vegeta-bles, but usually in small amounts. Tea and coconuts are other important crops. Fishing is an important industry in this region, and Sri Lankans eat more fish than red meat.

People and Language

Almost 75 percent of the Sri Lankan people are Sinhalese, who are descended from Aryan tribes. Another 18 percent of the people on Sri Lanka are Tamils, who are descended from Indians. Sin-halese is the official language of Sri Lanka, but Tamil is also widely spoken.

The two most common religions are Hinduism and Buddhism, which has elements of both Hin-duism and Islam. Religion plays an important role in Sri Lankan culture, and many religious festi-vals are celebrated throughout the year. Religion also affects the Sri Lankan people's food choices, since many Buddhists are strict vegetarians. Sri Lankans consider food to be a gift from the gods, and the first portion of a harvest is often given as an offering to the gods.

Dining

Sri Lankan cooking is known for its hot spiciness. Almost every Sri Lankan recipe calls for several kinds of spices! Along with spices, much of the island's cuisine is flavored with coconut. Fresh or dried coconut or, more commonly, coconut milk appears in many Sri Lankan specialties—including breads, desserts, rice, vegetables, and beef, chicken, and fish dishes.

Most Sri Lankan meals contain one or more *curries*—that is, meat or vegetables cooked in a curry sauce. Many people in western cultures think of curry as a powdered spice or a dish cooked with curry powder. In Sri Lanka, however, curry is more a method of cooking, involving a wide variety of seasonings. Therefore the spices blended in one curry may be different from those in another. An average curry might contain as many as 15 different spices.

In addition to the curries, a Sri Lankan meal usually includes one or two green vegetables and a large platter of rice. Typically, Sri Lankans place a serving of rice in the center of their plate and sur-round it with servings of the other foods. They then use the fingers of their right hand to mix the foods and eat the mixed foods.

(Continued on next page)

Port of Call: Sri Lanka (continued)

Sri Lankan Food Briefs

Sambols

There are hundreds of different kinds of Sri Lankan *sambols*—condiments used to add flavor to foods. Many sambols are extremely hot, while others are sweet and fruity. Most sambols have a paste-like texture, but some are dry and must be sprinkled on foods. A sambol is served at the table with the meal, and each person adds it to his or her food. Usually just one sambol is served per meal. The most traditional sambol is *seeni* (sugar) *sambol.* Seeni sambol contains onion, chilies, brown sugar, and dried, salted tuna, as well as numerous spices. Other sambols contain a wide variety of ingredients, including carrots, eggplant, coconut milk, hard-boiled eggs, limes, and pineapple.

Rottis

Rottis (pronounced row-tees) are pan-fried soft breads. Some rottis are made by wrapping dough around meat or vegetable mixtures and then frying. Depending upon their size, they may be served as a side dish or a main course. Sri Lankans usually serve these stuffed rottis with curries and sambols for dipping. Another type of popular rotti contains fresh or dried coconut. Many Sri Lankans eat these fried breads for breakfast.

Kiri Bath (Milk Rice)

This dish is a simple mixture of white rice and coconut milk cooked together. However, it is very important to the Sri Lankan people. Milk rice is traditionally cooked for breakfast on New Year's Day. In Sinhalese families, the rice mixture is allowed to boil over the top of the pot for good luck. It is considered especially lucky if the pot overflows on all sides. This means good fortune will come from all directions. Sri Lankans usually flavor their milk rice with either a hot sambol or *jaggery*—a coconut molasses similar to heavy brown sugar.

Looking Back on Sri Lanka

1. In Sri Lanka, a curried dish contains a variety of spices and a meat or vegetable combination. Invent your own curried dish by choosing a meat or vegetable(s) and deciding which spices you would like to add to it. If you need help choosing spices, use a cookbook or encyclopedia to research various kinds. Share your recipe with the class.

2. If you were served a dish in Sri Lanka that was unknown to you, what kind of overall taste would you expect? Why? Discuss your ideas in class.

3. List the foods of Sri Lanka that you would most like to try. Where can you find these foods? Which can you make?

4. The Sinhalese people have a New Year's Day tradition of eating milk rice for good luck. Which other cultures do you know of that view eating certain foods as tokens of good luck? Research this and write a newspaper article.

Dal
(Lentil Dish of India)

Dal
(Lentil Dish of India)

Customary	Ingredients	Metric
1 cup	Split, hulled lentils or yellow split peas	250 mL
2 cups	Water or vegetable broth	500 mL
1 tsp.	Salt	5 mL
2 Tbsp.	Vegetable oil	30 mL
1 tsp.	Black mustard seed (optional)	5 mL
1/3 cup	Chopped green pepper	75 mL
1/3 cup	Chopped onion	75 mL
1/2 tsp.	Turmeric	2 mL
1/2 tsp.	Curry powder	2 mL
2 tsp.	Lemon juice	10 mL
	Hot, cooked rice	

Yield: 4 servings

Directions

Pan: 1 1/2-qt. (1.5-L) saucepan; skillet

1. Combine lentils or split peas, water or broth, and salt in large saucepan. Bring to a boil. Reduce heat; simmer, covered, just until tender, about 30 minutes.

2. Heat vegetable oil in skillet. Add mustard seed. Cover and let seeds pop.

3. Stir in green pepper, onion, turmeric, and curry powder. Sauté until vegetables are soft, about 5 minutes.

4. Remove from heat. Stir in lemon juice.

5. Stir seasoned vegetable mixture into cooked lentils or split peas.

6. Serve with hot, cooked rice.

Nutrition Information: Serving size: 3/4 cup (175 mL) dal (no rice)

calories: 94	cholesterol: 0 mg	dietary fiber: 2 g
total fat: 7 g	sodium: 540 mg	sugars: 2 g
saturated fat: 1 g	carbohydrate: 7 g	protein: 2 g

Percent Daily Value: vitamin A 0%, vitamin C 22%, calcium 2%, iron 6%

Tip for Success

◆ Black mustard seeds have a different flavor from yellow ones and "pop" in hot oil. Look for them in Indian markets or natural food stores.

Curried Meat Patties

Curried Meat Patties

Customary	Ingredients	Metric
1 lb.	Ground beef or ground lamb	500 g
1	Egg	1
2 tsp.	Curry powder	10 mL
	Juice of $1/2$ lemon	
1	Green pepper, finely chopped	1
3 Tbsp.	Vegetable oil	45 mL
1	Onion, thinly sliced	1
1 Tbsp	Fresh coriander (cilantro), chopped	15 mL

Yield: 2 to 4 servings.

Directions

Pan: Medium skillet

1. Place meat, egg, curry powder, lemon juice, and green pepper in a bowl. Mix into a smooth paste.

2. Divide the mixture into four $1/2$-inch (1.25-cm) patties.

3. Heat the oil in a skillet over medium-high heat.

4. Add the patties and reduce the heat to medium. Fry the patties about 8 minutes on each side or until brown and cooked through.

5. Put patties on serving platter and decorate with the slices of onion and chopped coriander.

Nutrition Information: Serving size: $1/4$ to $1/2$ recipe

calories: 355
total fat: 27 g
saturated fat: 9 g
cholesterol: 123 mg
sodium: 83 mg

carbohydrate: 6 g
dietary fiber: 1 g
sugars: 3 g
protein: 22 g

Percent Daily Value: vitamin A 3%, vitamin C 39%, calcium 3%, iron 13%

Fish Curry

Fish Curry

Customary	Ingredients	Metric
2 Tbsp.	Vegetable oil	30 mL
1	Onion, finely chopped	1
1 clove	Garlic, finely chopped	1 clove
1/2 Tbsp.	Fresh ginger, finely chopped	7 mL
2	Tomatoes, chopped	2
1 tsp.	Ground turmeric	5 mL
1/2 Tbsp.	Ground cumin	7 mL
1 cup	Water	250 mL
1 lb.	Mild white fish fillets, such as orange roughy, catfish, or cod	500 g
1 1/4 oz.	Fresh coriander (cilantro), chopped	39 g
	salt (to taste)	

Yield: 4 servings

Directions

Pan: Large, heavy saucepan

1. Cut the fish into bite-size pieces and set aside.

2. Heat oil in saucepan. When oil is hot, add onions, garlic, and ginger. Cook, stirring, for 2 to 3 minutes.

3. Add tomatoes, ground turmeric, and ground cumin. Cook until tomatoes are soft.

4. Add water and bring to a boil.

5. Add fish and chopped coriander. Bring to a boil. Cover the saucepan, reduce heat to medium, and cook for 15 minutes.

Nutrition Information: Serving size: 1/4 recipe

calories: 240
total fat: 15 g
saturated fat: 1 g
cholesterol: 23 mg
sodium: 83 mg

carbohydrate: 8 g
dietary fiber: 1.4 g
sugars: 3 g
protein: 18 g

Percent Daily Value: vitamin A 3%, vitamin C 362%, calcium 44%, iron 88%

Mango and Coconut Chutney

Mango and Coconut Chutney

Customary	Ingredients	Metric
1 medium	Mango	1 medium
1 Tbsp.	Fresh ginger, finely chopped	15 mL
1/2 tsp.	Salt	2 mL
1/2 tsp.	Red pepper flakes	2 mL
1/4 cup	Coriander (cilantro), finely chopped	50 mL
1/2 cup	Coconut, shredded	125 mL

Yield: 4 servings

Directions

1. Cut mango into chunks.

2. Put all ingredients in a bowl and toss gently until completely mixed.

3. Refrigerate for at least one hour.

4. Serve as a condiment with curry.

Nutrition Information: Serving size: 1/4 recipe

calories: 85
total fat: 4 g
saturated fat: 4 g
cholesterol: 0 mg
sodium: 300 mg

carbohydrate: 15 g
dietary fiber: 1.7 g
sugars: 11 g
protein: 1 g

Percent Daily Value: vitamin A 21%, vitamin C 41%, calcium 2%, iron 6%

Touring Southwest Asia and North Africa
A Global Foods Tour

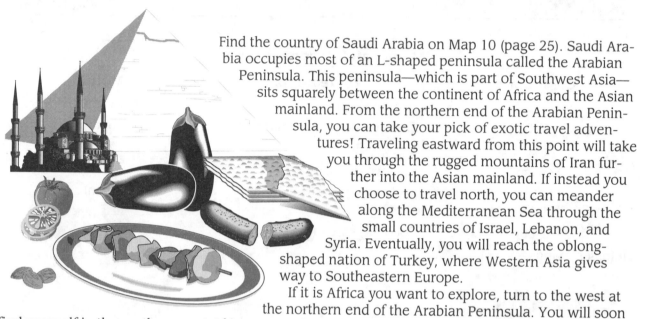

Find the country of Saudi Arabia on Map 10 (page 25). Saudi Arabia occupies most of an L-shaped peninsula called the Arabian Peninsula. This peninsula—which is part of Southwest Asia—sits squarely between the continent of Africa and the Asian mainland. From the northern end of the Arabian Peninsula, you can take your pick of exotic travel adventures! Traveling eastward from this point will take you through the rugged mountains of Iran further into the Asian mainland. If instead you choose to travel north, you can meander along the Mediterranean Sea through the small countries of Israel, Lebanon, and Syria. Eventually, you will reach the oblong-shaped nation of Turkey, where Western Asia gives way to Southeastern Europe.

If it is Africa you want to explore, turn to the west at the northern end of the Arabian Peninsula. You will soon find yourself in the northernmost African countries, where the landscape is the dry wasteland of the Sahara. The Sahara, which is the world's largest desert, stretches all the way across the top of Africa to the northwestern country of Morocco.

People and Cultures

Most of the people who live in Southwest Asia and North Africa are Arab people. Although they live in several countries and often have different traditions, all Arabs share two common bonds—language and religion. Most Arabs speak a variation of the Arabic language and follow the Islamic religion. The country of Israel is an exception in this Arab-populated region. More than 80 percent of Israel's people are Jewish. The religions of both the Jewish and the Arab peoples involve almost every aspect of their lives—including their food choices!

Cuisines of Southwest Asia and Northern Africa

Food choices and preparation methods in this part of the world are greatly affected by the dietary laws of the Islamic and the Judaic religions. Because followers of these religions cannot eat pork, for example, many foods that are common in other cultures are unheard of here. You will find no pepperoni pizzas, ham sandwiches, or sausage patties in this region. Lamb is the preferred meat. Southwest Asian and North African cuisines are also influenced by the available food supply. Olives, chickpeas, yogurt, goat's milk cheeses, nuts, and vegetables like tomatoes, cucumbers, and eggplant are key ingredients in many dishes.

The Savvy Gourmet

If you visit the nomadic Arab people who live in the desert, you will probably be served a thick, bitter coffee. When you are finished with your coffee, it is considered proper to shake the empty cup six times.

Port of Call

Egypt

Touring Southwest Asia and North Africa

Imagine you are taking a trip up the Nile River. Flowing from Lake Victoria in East Central Africa, the Nile snakes northward through Sudan and into Egypt. Here, the Nile is all-important. Without the broad, fertile valley created by this river, Egypt would be almost entirely desert. The Nile Valley turns into the Nile Delta in northern Egypt. The fertile, fan-shaped Delta starts about 100 miles (160 km) south of the Mediterranean Sea, where the Nile breaks into hundreds of smaller branches. The valley and delta together make up only 4 percent of Egypt, but this area is home to almost 99 percent of Egypt's people. The lush, green land around the Nile is some of the world's most productive farmland.

If you venture east or west out of the Nile Valley, you will find vast, empty stretches of desert. East of the Nile is the Arabian Desert, which runs all the way from the river to the Red Sea. The western two-thirds of Egypt are covered by the flat, sandy Western Desert, a part of the Sahara. Here, daytime temperatures reach 120 °F (49°C), while nights are often freezing. Few plants or animals can survive in this unfriendly land. The only parts of the desert that can grow crops are a handful of oases—areas that are naturally irrigated by underground rivers. In these oases, date palm trees and other crops grow well.

Food Traveler's Notes

Agriculture

The year-round warm weather and plentiful water supply of the Nile Valley and Delta allow Egyptian farmers to grow as many as three crops per year. The most important crops grown here are rice, tomatoes, wheat, corn, sugarcane, potatoes, oranges, and various other vegetables and fruits. Livestock raising is less important than crop farming.

People and Language

Most Egyptians are descended from the ancient Egyptian peoples and the Arabs who conquered the area in the seventh century. Arabic is the official language of the country. Approximately 40 percent of the 66 million people in Egypt are rural farmers, called *fellahin*. These fellahin live mostly in small villages, growing their own foods and leading lives that are much like those of their ancestors. Another 45 percent of Egyptians live in modern cities located along the Nile. No matter where or how they live, most Egyptians share a common religion—Islam. Islamic people are not allowed to eat pork. Because of this, sheep, poultry, and vegetables play important roles in most Egyptian meals.

Dining

Egyptians often eat five meals a day, but some of the meals are very light. Breakfast is often just a beverage and some beans and bread. Around mid-morning, people usually have another small meal, usually consisting of bread and perhaps cold meats, eggs, or pickles. Lunch is eaten in the afternoon and may be a simple meal of cheese, bread, and vegetables. When Egyptian families gather at home at the end of the day, they have another small meal—often some type of cooked meat and vegetables with rice. In wealthier homes, this meal may also include bread, salads, and olives. Egyptians eat their last meal around 10:00 P.M. This late supper usually consists of a bean dish, along with one or two side dishes.

(Continued on next page)

Egyptian Food Briefs

Foul (Fava Beans)

When visiting Egypt, you may find yourself eating fava beans at any time of the day or night! Egyptians prepare these protein-rich beans in a wide variety of ways. They may be boiled, then mashed with onions, tomatoes, and spices. When this same mixture is cooked down to a paste, it is used as a filling for sandwiches. Another popular way of preparing fava beans is to mix them with spices, form them into patties, and deep-fry them. These patties, topped with tomatoes, lettuce and a spicy sauce, are served with Egyptian bread called *aysh*. Egyptians even eat beans for breakfast, often cooked with butter and salt and sometimes served with an egg.

Pigeon

The bird that is considered a nuisance in many parts of the United States is considered a delicacy by the Egyptians. Pigeons are raised for food throughout Egypt—and sold everywhere from dusty market stalls to upscale restaurants as a special dinner treat. In rural areas, many families raise their own pigeons in a special structure called a *dovecote*. Egyptians prepare these small birds by stuffing them with seasoned rice or corn, then grilling or roasting them. They are usually served as a main course.

Sweet Pastries

Egyptian pastries are delicious, layered treats made of paper-thin phyllo dough and rich fillings. These pastries may be filled with a number of different ingredients, such as dried apricots, figs, or top-quality dates grown in the desert oases. Chopped nuts, raisins, and coconut are other popular fillings. For extra sweetness, pastries may be drenched in honey or syrup. Most Egyptians do not eat these treats for dessert after a meal. Instead, they have them as a snack, along with a cup of coffee or tea.

Looking Back on Egypt

1. Egyptian pastries are made of layers of dough combined with sweet fillings and often covered with honey or syrup. Imagine that you are a pastry chef and invent your own layered pastry. Write an entry for a restaurant menu describing your pastry and its filling.

2. Beans are a staple food in Egypt, eaten both by themselves and as part of various dishes. Using a cookbook, research recipes that feature beans. Briefly explain one that sounds appealing to you.

3. List the foods of Egypt that you would most like to try. Where can you find these foods? Which can you make?

4. Many Egyptians eat several small meals each day. Write a brief report discussing if it would be possible for people in your area to adopt this type of meal pattern. What factors might make doing so difficult? What might be the benefits of eating this way?

Port of Call

Israel

Touring Southwest Asia and North Africa

In the southwestern corner of Asia, right on the Mediterranean Sea, lies the narrow country of Israel. A wide variety of geographical features are packed into this small nation, which is slightly smaller than the state of New Jersey. At Israel's northernmost point, near its borders with Syria and Lebanon, is the Galilee region—a hilly agricultural area bordered on the east by the Jordan River and Lake Tiberias.

Traveling south from Galilee, you reach a long, thin stretch of plains, extending from the Mediterranean Sea eastward to Israel's border with Jordan. These coastal plains are home to most of Israel's major cities and the majority of its population. Here, the Mediterranean sunshine and rich soil create an excellent environment for farming. Citrus fruits, olives, grapes, and a wide array of vegetables thrive in this fertile region.

South of Israel's coastal plains region is the vast Negev Desert, which covers the southern half of the country. Although this region gets less than 10 inches of rain per year, modern irrigation techniques allow the Israelis to farm the land.

Food Traveler's Notes

Agriculture

Farming in Israel is very organized. Perhaps the most famous type of Israeli farms is the *kibbutz,* a cooperative farming village. On a kibbutz, all land and all property are owned jointly by the people who live and work there. Through Israel's many *kibbutzim* and similar farming methods, enough food is produced to feed almost all of Israel's population. The largest crops are citrus fruit, tomatoes, wheat, potatoes, melons, apples, and grapes. Cattle and sheep are the most important livestock.

People and Language

Of the 5.6 million people living in Israel, over 80 percent are Jewish. Although more than half of these Jewish people are Israeli-born, their parents and grandparents came from more than 100 different countries. In addition, more than 15 percent of Israel's people are Arabs. Therefore the culture, customs, and cuisine of Israel contain elements of Southwest Asia, Central and Eastern Europe, North Africa, and many other regions! When visiting a city in Israel, you might dine on such Middle Eastern foods as lamb shish kebobs or on such European specialties as smoked salmon and potato pancakes. Although Hebrew is the most common language here, visitors might also hear Arabic, English, Russian, or any number of other languages.

Dining

Israeli meals are greatly affected by the dietary laws of the country's two main religions, Judaism and Islam. The Jewish people, for example, cannot eat pork, shellfish, or any type of fish with scales. They are also not allowed to eat meat and dairy products at the same meal. The Islamic people, like the Jews, cannot eat pork.

Breakfast in Israel is typically hearty and may include cheese, vegetables, olives, and sometimes fish. Lunch is the main meal of the day for most people here. This meal is usually eaten later here than in Western cultures—around 3:00 P.M. when school is over for the day. Most Israelis eat a light dinner—often a salad or fish—around 7:00 in the evening.

(Continued on next page)

Israeli Food Briefs

Shakshouka

A favorite dish in Israel is *shakshouka*, an egg and tomato dish that originated in northern Africa. Although there are many slight variations of the recipe, traditional shakshouka is made by first sautéing tomato, onion, garlic, and various herbs. To complete this dish, Israelis poach eggs over the tomatoes and onion mixture. Some shakshouka recipes call for green peppers or pimentos as well.

Falafel

One of the most popular of all Israeli foods is *falafel*—deep-fried balls of a mixture of chickpeas, crushed wheat, and spices. Falafel is usually served in sandwich form, tucked into a flat, pocket-like bread called *pita*. However, the falafel balls can also be served as appetizers. Most Israelis serve falafel with a sauce made from either yogurt or *tahini*—a thick paste of ground sesame seeds. Falafel is now sold on practically every street corner in the towns and cities of Israel. Some people even call it the "Israeli hamburger!"

Matzo

Matzo is an unleavened bread, which means that it does not rise and get puffy, like yeast breads. Most Israeli people eat matzo during the Jewish holiday of Passover—a week-long celebration of the ancient Jewish people's escape from slavery in Egypt. The Jews eat unleavened bread during Passover as a reminder that their ancestors fled from Egypt so quickly that they couldn't wait for their bread to rise. Made only with flour and water, matzo is thin and brittle. Israelis often grind matzo into a powder and use it to thicken soups, to bread foods for frying, or to make pancakes or dumplings.

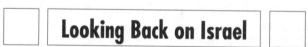

Looking Back on Israel

1. The food traditions of Jewish people in Israel and elsewhere are very detailed and strict. To help those among the Jewish people who choose to keep these traditions, Jewish food inspectors label foods that meet certain standards. The label may be the word *Kosher* or a symbol, such as the letter *k*, to indicate that the food is kosher. Conduct research to find other symbols for kosher and share your findings with the class.

2. *Challah bread, gefilte fish,* and *knishes* are some of the many traditional Jewish dishes common in the United States and elsewhere, as well as in Israel. Look for these and other Jewish foods in your grocery store and make a note of where are they made. Compare your list with your classmates'.

3. List the foods of Israel that you would most like to try. Where can you find these foods? Which can you make?

4. To celebrate Passover, the Jewish people eat a special meal called a *Seder*. Each type of food eaten at the Seder symbolizes something different about the holiday. Research the Seder and write a paragraph explaining what each food item symbolizes.

Egyptian Eggplant Omelet

Recipe 36

Touring Southwest Asia and North Africa

Egyptian Eggplant Omelet

Customary	Ingredients	Metric
1 large	Eggplant, peeled and cubed	1 large
2 to 6 Tbsp.	Butter or margarine	30 to 90 mL
1	Onion, finely chopped	1
1 clove	Garlic, finely chopped	1 clove
8	Eggs, lightly beaten	8
	Salt and pepper (to taste)	

Yield: 4 to 6 servings

Directions

Pan: Large skillet

1. Place cubed eggplant in a colander or strainer and sprinkle lightly with salt. Set in sink for 20 minutes to drain.

2. Rinse salt from eggplant under cold water. Drain eggplant and pat dry with paper towels.

3. In a skillet, over medium-high heat, melt 2 Tbsp. (30 mL) butter or margarine. Add onion and garlic and cook until onion is soft, about 3 minutes.

4. Reduce heat to medium, add eggplant and cook until eggplant is tender, about 6 minutes.

5. Add more butter or margarine to skillet to prevent sticking. Pour in eggs and season with salt and pepper. Mix thoroughly. Reduce heat to low; cover pan. Cook until eggs are firmly set, about 15 minutes.

6. Remove omelet from heat and flip it over onto a plate. Then slide it back into skillet, other side down. Cook for about 3 minutes. Cut into wedges to serve.

Nutrition Information: Serving size: $1/4$ to $1/6$ recipe

calories: 190
total fat: 14 g
saturated fat: 4 g
cholesterol: 284 mg
sodium: 174 mg

carbohydrate: 6 g
dietary fiber: 1.5 g
sugars: 2 g
protein: 9 g

Percent Daily Value: vitamin A 22%, vitamin C 3%, calcium 4%, iron 6%

Knishes with Potato Filling

(Jewish Baked Dumplings)

Recipe 37

Touring Southwest Asia and North Africa

Knishes with Potato Filling
(Jewish Baked Dumplings)

Customary	Ingredients	Metric
1 1/2 cups	Flour	350 mL
1/4 tsp.	Baking soda	1 mL
1/3 cup	Margarine, softened	75 mL
1/4 cup	Boiling water	50 mL
1/2 Tbsp.	Margarine	7 mL
2 Tbsp.	Onion, finely chopped	30 mL
One 5-oz.	Potato, cooked, peeled, and mashed	One 156-g
1/4 tsp.	Salt	1 mL
1/8 tsp.	Pepper	0.5 mL

Yield: 12 to 15 knishes

Directions

Pan: Skillet; baking sheet

1. Combine flour and baking soda in mixing bowl.

2. Cut in 1/3 cup (75 mL) margarine until crumbly.

3. Add boiling water and stir until dough is smooth.

4. Divide dough into two balls. Cover and refrigerate at least two hours.

5. Heat 1/2 Tbsp. (7 mL) margarine in skillet. Sauté onion in margarine for about 3 minutes.

6. Combine sautéed onion with mashed potato, salt, and pepper. Mix well. Set aside.

7. Preheat oven to 425°F (220°C). Grease baking sheet.

8. On lightly floured surface, roll out each ball of dough to 1/8 inch (3 mm) thickness. Cut out rounds of dough with 3-inch (8-cm) round cookie cutter dipped in flour.

9. Place 1 Tbsp. (15 mL) potato mixture in the center of each round. Dampen edges of dough with water, fold over filling, and press firmly to seal.

10. Place knishes on greased baking sheet. Bake at 425°F (220°C) until golden, about 20 minutes.

Nutrition Information: Serving size: 1 knish

calories: 90	cholesterol: 0 mg	dietary fiber: 0 g
total fat: 5 g	sodium: 101 mg	sugars: 0.4 g
saturated fat: 1 g	carbohydrate: 11 g	protein: 1 g

Percent Daily Value: vitamin A 6%, vitamin C 1%, calcium 0%, iron 3%

Baked Kibbe

(Lebanese Lamb and Bulgur Dish)

Recipe 38

Touring Southwest Asia and North Africa

Baked Kibbe
(Lebanese Lamb and Bulgur Dish)

Customary	Ingredients	Metric
$1/2$ cup	Bulgur	125 mL
1 cup	Water	250 mL
1 lb.	Lean ground lamb (divided)	500 g
1	Medium onion, chopped (divided)	1
$1/4$ cup	Pine nuts	50 mL
$1/2$ tsp.	Salt	2 mL
$1/4$ tsp.	Pepper	1 mL
$1/4$ tsp.	Cinnamon	1 mL
$1/4$ tsp.	Allspice	1 mL
$1/2$ tsp.	Salt	2 mL
$1/4$ tsp.	Pepper	1 mL
	Vegetable oil cooking spray	
2 Tbsp.	Olive oil or melted margarine	30 mL

Yield: 4 servings

Conventional Directions

Pans: Skillet; 8 x 8 inch (20 x 20 cm) baking pan

1. Place bulgur in bowl. Pour water over bulgur. Let stand 15 minutes.

2. Meanwhile, cook $1/2$ lb. (250 g) lamb and half the chopped onion in skillet about 3 minutes. Stir in pine nuts, $1/2$ tsp. (2 mL) salt, $1/4$ tsp. (1 mL) pepper, cinnamon, and allspice. Continue cooking until lamb is no longer pink. Set aside.

3. Drain bulgur well, using back of spoon to press out water. Mix in remaining raw lamb, remaining onion, $1/2$ tsp. (2 mL) salt, and $1/4$ tsp. (1 mL) pepper.

4. Coat bottom and sides of baking pan with cooking spray. Press half of raw lamb mixture into bottom of pan. Spread cooked lamb mixture over it. Make patties with remaining raw lamb, place over cooked

Microwave Directions

Pans: 1-qt. (1-L) casserole; 8 x 8 inch (20 x 20 cm) microwave-safe baking dish

1. Place bulgur in bowl. Pour water over bulgur. Let stand 15 minutes.

2. Meanwhile, place $1/2$ lb. (250 g) lamb and half the chopped onion in casserole. Microwave at 100% power for 3 to 4 minutes or until lamb is no longer pink. Stir in pine nuts, $1/2$ tsp. (2 mL) salt, $1/4$ tsp. (1 mL) pepper, cinnamon, and allspice. Set aside.

3. Drain bulgur well, using back of spoon to press out water. Mix in remaining raw lamb, remaining onion, $1/2$ tsp. (2 mL) salt, and $1/4$ tsp. (1 mL) pepper.

4. Coat bottom and sides of baking pan with cooking spray. Press half of raw lamb mixture into bottom of pan. Spread cooked lamb mixture over it. Make patties with

(Continued on next page)

Recipe 38 Baked Kibbe (continued)

Conventional (continued)

lamb mixture, and gently spread patties to fill gaps.

5. Use a wet, serrated knife to score the top layer with diagonal lines, forming a diamond pattern. Drizzle with olive oil or melted margarine.

6. Bake at 350°F (180°C) for 1 hour. Cut into pieces and serve.

Microwave (continued)

remaining raw lamb, place over cooked lamb mixture, and gently spread patties to fill gaps.

5. Use a wet, serrated knife to score the top layer with diagonal lines, forming a diamond pattern. Drizzle with olive oil or melted margarine.

6. Microwave at 100% power for 5 minutes

7. Rotate dish one-half turn. Microwave at 30% power for 17 to 20 minutes.

8. Let stand, covered, 5 minutes. Cut into pieces and serve.

Nutrition Information: Serving size: $1/4$ recipe

calories: 503
total fat: 38 g
saturated fat: 13 g
cholesterol: 84 mg
sodium: 608 mg

carbohydrate: 19 g
dietary fiber: 5 g
sugars: 2 g
protein: 23 g

Percent Daily Value: vitamin A 0%, vitamin C 4%, calcium 7%, iron 18%

Tips for Success

◆ "Kibbe" actually refers to the raw lamb and bulgur mixture. It can be prepared in many different ways.
◆ If you can't find ground lamb in the store, buy lean leg or shoulder of lamb. Ask to have it ground for you or grind it at home using a food processor.
◆ For easier handling, wet hands frequently while working with the kibbe.

Eggplant Salad with Yogurt Dressing

Recipe 39

Touring Southwest Asia and North Africa

Eggplant Salad with Yogurt Dressing

Customary	Ingredients	Metric
1 lb.	Eggplant	500 g
2 Tbsp.	Olive oil	30 mL
1 cup	Thinly sliced onion	250 mL
1 clove	Garlic, minced	1 clove
1 cup	Green pepper, sliced	250 mL
16-oz. can	Tomatoes, drained and cut into chunks	500-g can
1 Tbsp.	Lemon juice	15 mL
4 leaves	Leaf lettuce	4 leaves
	Yogurt Dressing (recipe follows)	
	Sliced, pitted black olives (optional)	

Yield: 4 servings

Conventional Directions

Pan: Skillet

1. Cut eggplant in half lengthwise. Cut each half into $1/2$ inch (1.25 cm) slices. Sprinkle lightly with salt. Let stand on paper toweling for 30 minutes to draw out excess moisture. Rinse off salt; pat eggplant dry with paper toweling.

2. Heat olive oil in skillet. Sauté garlic and onion until softened.

3. Add eggplant slices to skillet. Cook over low heat, covered, until eggplant is tender.

4. Stir in green pepper and tomato. Remove from heat.

5. Transfer salad to heat-resistant serving bowl. Drizzle lemon juice over salad. Cover and refrigerate 1 hour or longer.

6. Serve on salad plates lined with lettuce leaves. Top with Yogurt Dressing. Garnish with olive slices, if desired.

Microwave Directions

Pan: 2-qt. (2-L) microwave-safe casserole

1. Follow Step 1 of conventional directions.

2. Combine olive oil, garlic, and onion in casserole. Cover. Microwave at 100% power for 1 minute.

3. Add eggplant slices; cover. Microwave at 100% power for 5 to 7 minutes or until eggplant is tender, stirring once.

4. Stir in green pepper and tomato. Continue with Step 5 of conventional directions.

(Continued on next page)

Recipe 39 Eggplant Salad (continued)

Yogurt Dressing

Customary	Ingredients	Metric
1 cup	Plain low-fat or nonfat yogurt	250 mL
1 clove	Garlic, pressed	1 clove
1 tsp.	Paprika	5 mL
1/2 tsp.	Lemon juice	2 mL
1/4 tsp.	Salt	1 mL
	Pepper to taste	

Yield: 1 cup

Directions

1. Combine all ingredients and stir until well blended.

2. Serve with Eggplant Salad.

Nutrition Information: Serving size: 1/4 salad recipe plus 1 Tbsp. (15 mL) dressing

calories: 140
total fat: 7 g
saturated fat: 1 g
cholesterol: 0 mg
sodium: 194 mg

carbohydrate: 18 g
dietary fiber: 5 g
sugars: 8 g
protein: 3 g

Percent Daily Value: vitamin A 11%, vitamin C 67%, calcium 6%, iron 9%

Blintzes
(Thin Pancakes with Cheese Fillings)

Blintzes
(Thin Pancakes with Cheese Fillings)

Customary	Ingredients	Metric
3/4 cup	Dry cottage cheese	175 mL
1 Tbsp.	Cornstarch	15 mL
2 Tbsp.	Sugar	30 mL
1/2 tsp.	Grated lemon rind	2 mL
3/4 cup	All-purpose flour	175 mL
1 Tbsp.	Cornstarch	15 mL
1/8 tsp.	Salt	0.5 mL
1 cup	Fat-free milk	250 mL
1	Egg	1
1/2 tsp.	Vanilla	2 mL
	Vegetable oil cooking spray	
1 tsp.	Margarine	5 mL
	Sugar and cinnamon (optional)	

Yield: 12 blintzes

Directions

Pan: 6-inch (15-cm) skillet

1. Blend dry cottage cheese, 1 Tbsp. (15 mL) cornstarch, sugar, and grated lemon rind until smooth. Set aside.

2. Combine flour, 1 Tbsp. (15 mL) cornstarch, and salt in a medium mixing bowl.

3. Add milk, egg, and vanilla to dry ingredients. Blend well to make a thin batter.

4. Coat skillet with cooking spray. Heat skillet over medium-low heat.

5. Pour 1/4 cup (50 mL) batter into skillet. Tilt skillet so batter coats bottom evenly. Cook until pancake is browned on bottom, about 2 minutes.

6. Turn pancake and cook about 1 minute longer. Transfer to a plate and cover with waxed paper.

7. Repeat steps 5 and 6 with remaining batter.

8. Place 1 Tbsp. (15 mL) cheese mixture in the center of one pancake. Fold sides of pancake over the filling, overlapping the edges. Fold ends toward center, overlapping the edges, to form a rectangle. Repeat with remaining blintzes.

9. Heat margarine in skillet. Place blintzes in skillet, seam side down, and brown lightly, 1 to 2 minutes on each side.

(Continued on next page)

Recipe 40 Blintzes (continued)

10. Serve warm, dusted with cinnamon and sugar, if desired.

Nutrition Information: Serving size: 1 blintz

calories: 63
total fat: 1 g
saturated fat: 0 g
cholesterol: 19 mg
sodium: 43 mg

carbohydrate: 10 g
dietary fiber: 0 g
sugars: 3 g
protein: 4 g

Percent Daily Value: vitamin A 3%, vitamin C 0%, calcium 3%, iron 2%

Tips for Success

◆ If dry cottage cheese is not available, substitute creamed cottage cheese, draining off as much liquid as possible.
◆ You may want to use a larger skillet for browning the filled blintzes so that you can brown more of them at a time.

Hummus bi Tahini

(Garbanzo Spread with Tahini)

Recipe 41

Touring Southwest Asia and North Africa

Hummus bi Tahini
(Garbanzo Spread with Tahini)

Customary	Ingredients	Metric
1 cup	Canned garbanzo beans (chick-peas), drained and rinsed	250 mL
1/4 cup	Tahini (sesame paste)	50 mL
2 Tbsp.	Lemon juice	30 mL
1 clove	Garlic, minced	1 clove
Dash	Salt	Dash
1 Tbsp.	Minced parsley	15 mL
	Pita bread	

Yield: About 1 1/4 cups (300 mL)

Directions

1. Puree beans in a blender (or mash with fork).

2. Add tahini, lemon juice, garlic, and salt. Blend until smooth.

3. Place mixture in a serving bowl. Garnish with minced parsley.

4. Serve as a spread or dip with pita bread.

Nutrition Information: Serving size: 1/4 cup (50 mL)

calories: 114
total fat: 7 g
saturated fat: 1 g
cholesterol: 0 mg
sodium: 260 mg

carbohydrate: 9 g
dietary fiber: 3 g
sugars: 0 g
protein: 5 g

Percent Daily Value: vitamin A 0%, vitamin C 9%, calcium 2%, iron 8%

Tips for Success

◆ Tahini is sold in the ethnic food section of many supermarkets.
◆ If the mixture is too thick, add a little water to make a spreadable consistency.
◆ The pita bread may be cut into strips or triangles for easier eating.

Touring Africa South of the Sahara

A Global Foods Tour

If you won a trip to Africa, what would you expect to see? Miles of desert sand dunes? Hot, wet, jungles? Grasslands filled with exotic grazing animals? Depending on which part of this second-largest of continents you visit, you might see any of these. Africa has them all and more. Look at Map 11 (page 26). The northern part of Africa is covered with diagonally striped lines that represent the Sahara—the world's largest desert. The countries that lie south of the Sahara are referred to as Sub-Saharan countries or simply as countries south of the Sahara. The island of Madagascar, which lies off the southeastern African coast, is also part of this region. As you can see on the map, the largest country of this region is the Democratic Republic of the Congo, which was formerly known as Zaire. It is here that you will find one of the world's largest and thickest tropical rain forests. Wondering about those grasslands? They begin just south of the Sahara and wrap around the Congo Basin, which houses that large rain forest. The Kalahari Desert is one of Africa's wildlife paradises.

People and Cultures

The Sub-Saharan region contains the majority of Africa's 642 million inhabitants. The people of this area are extremely diverse, with more than 3,000 different ethnic groups and more than 1,000 different languages! Although most of the Sub-Saharan people are black Africans, there are also about 5 million people of European descent and about 1 million Indian people.

Although there are major cities, most of the region is rural. The majority of Africans are farmers and herders who raise crops and livestock for their own families. Social life in these rural areas generally centers on the family and the *kin group*—a group of people who share common ancestry. A whole African village is often made up of a single kin group.

Cuisines of Africa South of the Sahara

Many people rely on grains, corn, and legumes for most of their diet. Other common foods in the region include yams, okra, peanuts, and tropical fruits. Along coastal areas, seafood is also common.

Many African people eat only one real meal a day and have snacks in place of the other meals. An African meal typically consists of only one dish, instead of a main dish plus side dishes. This main dish is usually some combination of spiced meat and vegetables, served with bread, rice, or porridge. Fresh fruit is the most common dessert in most parts of Africa.

The Savvy Gourmet

Dairy cattle cannot be raised in many areas of central Africa, because of the presence of *tsetse flies*—insects that carry a deadly disease. In these regions, expect to find canned margarine, cheese, and powdered milk used to substitute for fresh dairy products.

Port of Call

South Africa

Touring Africa South of the Sahara

Taking up an area about twice the size of the state of Texas, South Africa occupies the southern-most tip of Africa. On the northern border of South Africa are the countries of Namibia, Botswana, Zimbabwe, Mozambique, and Swaziland. The rest of South African soil ends at water's edge—at the Indian Ocean on the east and south and at the Atlantic Ocean on the west. Open, grassy plateau areas, called the *veld,* cover about two-thirds of the country, separated by mountain chains from the long South African coastline. Most of the country has a warm, comfortable climate, with long sunny days and cool nights. There is little rain in South Africa, and drought is a common problem in many parts.

South Africa is rich in precious metals and gemstones, and parts of the country are peppered with gold and diamond mines. The mining industry here is one of the most advanced in the world. South Africa is also more urbanized than many other sub-Saharan countries. Around 60 percent of the total population lives in cities.

Food Traveler's Notes

Agriculture

Only about 10 percent of the land in South Africa is good for farming. The largest crop is corn, which is the staple food of many South Africans. South African farmers also raise wheat, sugarcane, fruits, and vegetables. Chicken and eggs are the most important livestock products, followed by cattle and dairy products. Fish and shellfish are important foods, especially on the west coast, which has excellent fishing waters.

People and Language

South Africa is shared by three main population groups. The largest group is the native South Africans, who make up more than 75 percent of the total population in South Africa. There are several smaller ethnic subgroups within the native population, and most of these groups have their own languages. The second major population group is made up of descendants of Dutch, German, French, British, and Portuguese colonists. These European groups settled in South Africa in the 17th century, establishing their own community and language—*Afrikaans.* The third major South African group is the *Coloured people*—people of mixed native African, Asian, and European ancestry. Most of the Coloured people speak Afrikaans.

Dining

The cuisine and dining customs of South Africans are an interesting combination of several cultures. The many different European peoples who settled in South Africa through the years brought their own foods and food preparation methods. These European cuisines combined with the native cuisine to create today's unique South African blend of flavors and food customs.

In rural areas of South Africa, meals are typically very simple. Food is usually served in clay pots on mats spread on the floor. A typical dinner might be a thick cornmeal porridge topped with a spicy stew. Dining in the urban areas of South Africa, however, is often similar to dining in western cultures. Food may be served on china dishes, and meals often include appetizers, soup, and several different dishes. Wherever you eat in South Africa, you will almost certainly be served some form of corn—which the South Africans call *mealies.*

(Continued on next page)

South African Food Briefs

Bobotie

Although South Africa is known for this meat and custard dish, it was actually invented in Malaysia. It was introduced into South Africa in the 17th century when Dutch settlers brought Malaysian slaves into the area. Traditional *bobotie* is a combination of curried lamb or beef mixed with raisins, sugar, apple, and almonds, topped with an egg custard. Many bobotie recipes call for lemon slices or lemon leaves to be used as a garnish. Other variations of this dish include apricots, orange juice, and cider vinegar. South Africans serve bobotie warm, with a bowl of rice and sometimes with sliced banana and toasted coconut!

Rock lobster

Rock lobster is the type of lobster found in the waters off the coast of South Africa. Because a rock lobster has no claws, almost all of its meat is in the tail. South Africans prepare this delicacy in a number of different ways and serve it as an appetizer or a main course. One of the most common dishes is rock lobster tail salad, which includes celery, honeydew melon, mayonnaise, and various spices.

Sosaties

If an Afrikaner asks you to a *braai*—the Afrikaans word for barbecue—you will probably get to sample *sosaties.* Sosaties are the South African version of shish kebabs, and they are traditional barbecue food. To make sosaties, South Africans marinate small pieces of lamb in a mixture of onion, brown sugar, apricot jam, and various spices for two to three days. The lamb pieces are then placed on a skewer and grilled over hot coals. The sosaties are served with a hot apricot sauce, rice, and crisp biscuits. In addition to lamb, some South African cooks grill dried apricots that have been marinated.

Looking Back on South Africa

1. Typical meals in the large cities of South Africa differ from those eaten in the rural villages. Do you think this is typical of other countries? Explain your answer.

2. All three of the South African dishes listed in the Food Briefs combine a fruit with a meat. Can you think of dishes in your culture that combine fruit with meat? List the dishes and fruits and meats they contain.

3. List the foods of South Africa that you would most like to try. Where can you find these foods? Which can you make?

4. *Sosaties* are a traditional barbecue food in South Africa. Write a menu of foods that are traditional at barbecues, cookouts, or picnics in your culture.

Name _____ Date _____ Class _____

Port of Call

Kenya

Touring Africa South of the Sahara

The country of Kenya lies on Africa's east edge and has a short strip of coastline on the warm Indian Ocean. The rest of Kenya is bordered by the neighboring African nations of Ethiopia, Somalia, Sudan, Uganda, and Tanzania. The eastern parts of Kenya are mostly flat. As you travel west, however, the land gets gradually higher and hillier until it reaches a series of volcanic mountain ranges in the western part of the country. Through these western mountain chains runs the Great Rift Valley—a deep valley that runs all the way from the top to the bottom of eastern Africa.

The equator cuts through the middle of Kenya like a belt, dividing it into two almost equal parts. Therefore any part of the country you visit is likely to be quite warm. Although the northern regions are extremely dry, parts of southern Kenya are tropical and humid. A dense bamboo rain forest covers the south and southeastern areas.

In Kenya you will find all the big game animals you might expect to see on an African safari. Here, elephants, rhinoceroses, zebras, giraffes, and lions all roam the grassy plains. Exotic tropical birds are plentiful too, as well as snakes such as pythons and cobras.

Food Traveler's Notes

Agriculture

Even though only 4 percent of Kenya is farmland, farmers produce a wide variety of foods. Among the many crops grown here are sugarcane, corn, pineapples, potatoes, grains, beans, and peanuts. Beef cattle and dairy products are other important agricultural products.

People and Language

Almost all of the 28 million Kenyans are native Africans, divided into more than 30 ethnic groups, or tribes. Most of these 30 tribes have their own languages, although many of the languages are similar to each other. Many Kenyans also speak Swahili—a mix of Arabic, Asian, European, and African tribal languages. Swahili is the official language of Kenya.

Most Kenyans are farmers and ranchers. They live primarily in the southern and western areas of the country, which get the most rain and so are best for farming. Within most Kenyan tribes, the family is the center of social life. Family members and friends often visit each other and are always greeted warmly! Hospitality is important to the Kenyans, and they take great care to make sure that their guests feel welcomed and comfortable.

Dining

Eating habits vary from tribe to tribe in Kenya. In one tribe, for example, men are usually served first. Adults and children may eat separately. In many parts of Kenya, people eat traditional African foods with the fingers of their right hand. For European foods, however, a knife and a fork are often used. To pass and accept items, Kenyans use the right hand or both hands. It is considered improper to use the left hand alone.

A typical Kenyan meal might start with soup, served in small bowls. After the soup, all the remaining foods are served at once, in brightly decorated bowls called calabashes. Often, a meal consists simply of a starch, such as porridge or rice, and a meat or vegetable stew. In Kenya, as in most of Africa, desserts are usually fruit. A juicy papaya is a favorite choice!

(Continued on next page)

Port of Call: Kenya (continued)

Kenyan Food Briefs

Ugali

For many Kenyans, *ugali*—a very stiff cornmeal porridge—is the most important food. This simple but filling food is a part of many Kenyan meals and is often served with a vegetable stew or meat with gravy. To eat a serving of ugali in a traditional way, Kenyans use their thumb to press a hole in the middle of it. They use this hole as a "bowl" for sauces and stews. For breakfast, Kenyans add milk or water to ugali to make it thinner and soupier.

Groundnut (Peanut) Stew

Chicken and peanuts—called *"groundnuts"* by the Kenyans—form the base for this regional specialty. To prepare the thick, delicious groundnut stew, Kenyan cooks first grind their own peanuts by pounding them with a wooden pestle. When the peanuts are ground into a paste, they are then mixed with hot chicken broth. This mixture is combined with cooked chicken and onions. Some recipes also include tomatoes, eggplant, green peppers, or other vegetables. Kenyans serve groundnut stew over plates of rice or porridge.

Coconut Dishes

The coconuts that grow in the coastal areas off the Indian Ocean provide the flavor for a wide range of Kenyan dishes. For example, Kenyans may serve fish with coconut or chicken in a rich coconut milk sauce. Coconut is added to vegetable dishes too. One spicy vegetable dish is made of red beans, chili peppers, tomatoes, onions, and coconut milk. A thick coconut rice dish, *wali wa nazi,* is often served with chicken, fish, or vegetables. For a sweeter dish, Kenyans may cook sliced *plantains* (a type of banana) in coconut milk spiced with cinnamon and clove.

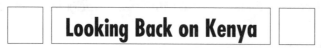

Looking Back on Kenya

1. Coconut and coconut milk are often used in Kenyan cooking. Research the nutrition information for coconut. What nutrients does it provide? Prepare a chart showing how it compares nutritionally to cow's milk.

2. In Kenya, certain foods are eaten in certain ways. For example, to eat ugali, Kenyans make a hole in it with their thumb and fill the hole with stew or sauce. In the United States, as well, certain foods are eaten in certain ways. Corn on the cob, for example, is usually eaten by hand, right off the cob. Brainstorm with your classmate other foods that are eaten in certain ways in your culture.

3. List the foods of Kenya that you would most like to try. Where can you find these foods? Which can you make?

4. In Kenya, it is considered impolite to pass and accept foods using only your left hand. Write a short story illustrating things that are considered impolite in your own culture.

Peanut Soup

Peanut Soup

Customary	Ingredients	Metric
4 cups	Chicken broth (divided)	1 L
3/4 cup	Chunky peanut butter	175 mL
2 Tbsp.	Margarine	30 mL
2 Tbsp.	All-purpose flour	30 mL
	Pepper (to taste)	
	Chopped fresh parsley (optional)	

Yield: 6 servings

Conventional Directions

Pan: $1^1/_2$-qt. (1.5-L) saucepan

1. In a medium bowl, stir 2 cups (500 mL) chicken broth into peanut butter until well combined. Set aside.

2. Melt margarine in large saucepan over low heat.

3. Stir flour into margarine. Cook, stirring constantly, about 2 minutes.

4. Gradually stir in remaining 2 cups (500 mL) broth. Increase heat; bring to a boil, stirring slowly and constantly.

5. Stir in peanut butter mixture until smooth.

6. Reduce heat to low. Let soup simmer 10 minutes.

7. Season with pepper. Garnish with parsley, if desired.

Microwave Directions

Pan: 2-qt. (2-L) glass casserole

1. In a medium bowl, stir 2 cups (500 mL) chicken broth into peanut butter until well combined. Set aside.

2. Place margarine in casserole. Microwave at 100% power for 45 seconds or until melted.

3. Stir flour into margarine. Microwave at 100% power for 30 seconds.

4. Stir in remaining 2 cups (500 mL) broth. Microwave at 100% power for 6 to 8 minutes, stirring every 2 minutes.

5. Stir in peanut butter mixture until smooth.

6. Microwave at 100% power for 4 to 6 minutes or until heated through, stirring twice.

7. Season with pepper. Garnish with parsley, if desired.

Nutrition Information: Serving size: $^1/_6$ recipe

calories: 258
total fat: 20 g
saturated fat: 4 g
cholesterol: 0 mg
sodium: 718 mg

carbohydrate: 9 g
dietary fiber: 2 g
sugars: 0 g
protein: 11 g

Percent Daily Value: vitamin A 5%, vitamin C 0%, calcium 2%, iron 7%

Kenyan Greens with Lemon Sauce

Recipe 43

Touring Africa South of the Sahara

Kenyan Greens with Lemon Sauce

Customary	Ingredients	Metric
2 lb.	Fresh greens (kale, collards, or spinach)	1 kg
1³/₄ cups	Water	425 mL
2 Tbsp.	Vegetable oil	30 mL
1	Onion, chopped	1
2	Tomatoes, chopped	2
2¹/₂ Tbsp.	Fresh lemon juice	37 mL
1 Tbsp.	All-purpose flour	15 mL
¹/₂ tsp.	Salt	2 mL

Yield: 4 to 6 servings

Directions

Pan: Large skillet

1. Rinse greens well, drain, and pat dry with paper towels.

2. Remove and discard the thick stems. Stack leaves a few at a time and cut them into 1/2-inch (1.25-cm) wide strips.

3. Pour 1 cup (250 mL) water into a large skillet and bring to a boil.

4. Add the greens, cover, and cook over medium heat, stirring frequently. Cook until greens are barely tender, about 10 minutes.

5. Remove greens. Drain thoroughly.

(Continued on next page)

Recipe 43 Kenyan Greens (continued)

6. Dry the frying pan and use it to heat the oil. Add onion and cook about 5 minutes, stirring often.

7. Add tomatoes and cook for 2 minutes. Stir in the drained greens.

8. In a medium bowl, blend together until smooth the remaining 3/4 cup (175 mL) water, lemon juice, flour, and salt. Stir mixture into greens and reduce heat to low.

9. Simmer, stirring often, until the sauce has thickened.

Nutrition Information: Serving size: 1/4 to 1/6 recipe

calories: 114
total fat: 5 g
saturated fat: 0.7 g
cholesterol: 0 mg
sodium: 219 mg

carbohydrate: 14 g
dietary fiber: 6 g
sugars: 5 g
protein: 4 g

Percent Daily Value: vitamin A 114%, vitamin C 123%, calcium 11%, iron 9%

Fufu
(Yam Balls)

Fufu
(Yam Balls)

Customary	**Ingredients**	**Metric**
Two 12-oz.	Yams	Two 375-g

Yield: About 16 yam balls
(4 servings)

Directions

1. Scrub yams and cut into quarters.

2. Cook yams by one of the following methods until easily pierced with a fork.

   ◆ Microwave on a paper towel at 100% for 6 to 8 minutes (or according to directions in oven manual or cooking guide).

   ◆ Place in steamer basket over boiling water; cover and steam about 20 minutes.

3. Let yams cool until they can be handled.

4. Scoop flesh out into a large bowl. Mash thoroughly.

5. With wet hands, shape mashed yams into balls about $1^1/_2$ inches (4 cm) in diameter.

6. Serve fufu immediately, as an accompaniment to meat or on top of a stew or soup.

Nutrition Information: Serving size: $^1/_4$ recipe

calories: 196
total fat: 0 g
saturated fat: 0 g
cholesterol: 0 mg
sodium: 13 mg

carbohydrate: 47 g
dietary fiber: 2 g
sugars: 0.8 g
protein: 3 g

Percent Daily Value: vitamin A 0%, vitamin C 34%, calcium 2%, iron 5%

West African Yellow Rice

Recipe 45

Touring Africa South of the Sahara

West African Yellow Rice

Customary	Ingredients	Metric
1 1/2 cups	Water	350 mL
1/2 cup	Orange juice	125 mL
1 cup	Long-grain rice	250 mL
1/3 cup	Seedless raisins	75 mL
2 Tbsp.	Sugar	30 mL
1 tsp.	Ground turmeric	5 mL
1/4 tsp.	Salt	1 mL
1 Tbsp.	Margarine	15 mL

Yield: 6 servings

Directions

Pan: 1-qt. (1-L) saucepan

1. Combine water and orange juice in saucepan. Bring to a boil.

2. Add rice, raisins, sugar, turmeric, salt, and margarine. Stir to combine. Cover and bring to a boil again.

3. Reduce heat. Simmer, covered, until liquid is absorbed and rice is cooked, about 15 minutes.

4. Fluff with fork. Serve hot.

Nutrition Information: Serving size: about 1/2 cup (125 g)

calories: 179
total fat: 2 g
saturated fat: 0 g
cholesterol: 0 mg
sodium: 116 mg

carbohydrate: 37 g
dietary fiber: 1 g
sugars: 11 g
protein: 3 g

Percent Daily Value: vitamin A 3%, vitamin C 17%, calcium 2%, iron 11%

Tip for Success

◆ Turmeric gives this dish its yellow color. If you wish, you can create a variation of the recipe by substituting another spice, such as ground cinnamon.

Injera
(Flat Ethiopian Bread)

Injera
(Flat Ethiopian Bread)

Customary	Ingredients	Metric
1 tsp.	Vegetable oil	5 mL
1/2 cup	Whole wheat flour	125 mL
1/4 cup	All-purpose flour	50 mL
3/4 tsp.	Baking powder	4 mL
1/4 tsp.	Salt	1 mL
1 cup	Water	250 mL

Yield: 6 servings

Directions

Pan: 6-inch (15-cm) nonstick skillet

1. Heat oil in skillet over medium heat.

2. Combine flours, baking powder, and salt in mixing bowl.

3. Gradually stir in water to form a slightly lumpy batter.

4. Pour 1/3 cup (75 mL) batter into hot skillet, tilting skillet to spread batter evenly on bottom.

5. Cook until small bubbles form and break on edges of bread, about 1 to 2 minutes. Turn bread and cook 1 to 2 minutes longer.

6. Repeat steps 4 and 5 using remaining batter.

7. Serve bread immediately, or stack on plate and cover to keep warm.

Nutrition Information: Serving size: 1 piece

calories: 59
total fat: 1 g
saturated fat: 0 g
cholesterol: 0 mg
sodium: 132 mg

carbohydrate: 11 g
dietary fiber: 1 g
sugars: 0.2 g
protein: 2 g

Percent Daily Value: vitamin A 0%, vitamin C 0%, calcium 1%, iron 4%

Tip for Success

◆ Traditionally, injera is used as an edible utensil. It is folded or rolled and used to scoop food, such as stew, from the serving dish.

Touring Australia and Oceania

A Global Foods Tour

If you travel directly southeast from the Asian nation of Vietnam, leapfrogging over the Indonesian Islands, you will find yourself in Australia. Look at Map 1 (page 16) to locate this island nation, which is the largest part of the region of the world called Oceania. To the east of Australia, is the mountainous country of New Zealand. The rest of Oceania, which fans out to the east of Australia and New Zealand, is thousands of tiny islands sprinkled through the blue waters of the South Pacific.

The Oceanic islands are actually the tops of underwater mountains, so when you have dinner on an island here, you are dining on a mountaintop! The largest of these islands is New Guinea, which is about the size of the state of California and is divided between the independent nation of Papua New Guinea to the east and a part of Indonesia called Irian Jaya to the west. Many of the Oceanic islands, however, are tiny, rugged, and volcanic, with not a single inhabitant. The islands of Oceania are split into three groups, based on the cultural characteristics of the people who live on them: Melanesia, Micronesia, and Polynesia.

People and Cultures

Scattered groups of people live throughout the Oceanic Islands. Most of these people live in small, independent villages in rural areas. Because the Oceanic people are so separated from each other by water and miles, the individual groups have little in common. A great number of different languages and customs can be found in this large island-filled region.

The first known people to live in Australia are the Aborigines. In the 18th century, however, the British began to colonize the country. Today, most Australians are European immigrants or descendants of European immigrants. English is Australia's official language.

Cuisines of Australia and Oceania

The diverse people of Oceania and Australia have one thing in common—they are excellent farmers and herders. As such, they produce most of their own foods. Cuisines throughout the Oceanic islands vary, depending upon which foods are most commonly grown. For example, some Micronesian islands produce large quantities of rice, taro, and the starchy breadfruit. These foods are mealtime staples on these islands. Polynesians and Melanesians rely on yams, coconut, pigs, and fish for much of their food. In Australia and New Zealand, where livestock is very important, many dishes feature beef, lamb, and dairy products.

The Savvy Gourmet

Eating a formal meal in Australia can be challenging to visitors! To eat in the formal Australian fashion, you must always hold the fork in your left hand, with the fork tines pointing down instead of up.

Port of Call

Australia

Touring Australia and Oceania

Australia is nicknamed "the land down under" because it lies completely south of the equator. At approximately the size of the United States, it is also the smallest continent in the world, and the only continent that is also a country. As you can see on Map 12 (page 27), Australia's nearest neighbors are the islands of New Guinea and New Zealand.

The interior of Australia is its famous Outback—the enormous bush-covered wilderness that is home to such wildlife as kangaroos, koala bears, and dingoes (wild dogs). Although the Outback is perhaps the best known part of the country, very few Australians live there. About four-fifths of all Australians live along the country's southern and eastern coastal areas.

These coastal areas have the most moderate climates of any part of Australia—with cool winters, warm summers, and enough rainfall to make for good farming. It is in these temperate areas that most of Australia's largest crops are raised. Beef and dairy cattle, which are an important part of the Australian food supply, thrive in this region too.

Food Traveler's Notes

Agriculture

Livestock is the most important part of Australian agriculture. Millions of sheep, beef cattle, and dairy cattle are raised here, mostly in the eastern parts of the country. Because meat is plentiful in Australia, it makes up a large part of daily meals.

Only about 6 percent of the land in Australia is used to grow crops. Sugarcane and grains, such as wheat and barley, are the most important crops. Grapes, oranges, apples, bananas, pears, pineapples, and peaches are raised in the southern and eastern regions.

People and Language

The people of Australia have a unique and interesting heritage. The original Australians were a tribal group of people called the Aborigines. The Aborigines settled in Australia more than 40,000 years ago, traveling from place to place and living only on foods they could hunt or gather. In the 18th century, the British immigrants settled in Australia. Today, Australia is made up mostly of English-speaking descendants of early British settlers. Approximately 240,000 Aborigines remain—some of whom still live in traditional tribal ways.

Dining

Receiving an invitation to tea in Australia can be confusing. In many areas, "tea" refers to the evening meal. In addition, Australians have "morning tea" and "afternoon tea." Morning tea, which consists of tea and cookies, is usually served around 10:30 A.M. Although morning tea is an everyday meal, afternoon tea is more likely to be served only weekends.

Australians do not serve food in the family style that is so common in the United States. Instead of putting serving dishes on the table to be passed around, Australians fill the diners' plates with food in the kitchen and then bring them to the table. Meals usually feature meat served with potatoes and vegetables. Typically, Australians do not like spicy food.

The immigrants from mainland Europe have influenced Australian cuisine. Italian, Greek, and other European styles of cooking have caught on in the land down under. Asian food is also popular, and Chinese, Indonesian, and Vietnamese restaurants are found in the larger cities.

(Continued on next page)

Australian Food Briefs

Barbecue

Much Australian cuisine features choice cuts of meat—especially lamb and beef. By far the most popular way to prepare these meats is on the barbecue—called a *barbie.* Although lamb and beef are the most common grill foods, Australians barbecue almost any kind of meat, including chicken, sausages, and seafood. A favorite barbecued meal is the "mixed grill," a heavy, hearty mixture of grilled steak, sausage, and lamb, served with fried bacon and sautéed mushrooms. Australians often serve a mixed grill with Aussie chips (french fries).

Bush Tucker

Tucker is the Australian word for food, and *bush tucker* refers to the kinds of foods that can be found wild in the Outback. Although the Aborigines have been eating bush tucker for more than 40,000 years, it may not appeal to the average traveler. One of the most common kinds of bush tucker is the *witchety grub,* a fat, white larvae. These grubs are a staple food of the Outback Aborigines, who eat them raw or rolled in ashes. Brave Australians and visitors prefer to eat them cooked, with salt and pepper and yams. Other bush foods include kangaroo, roast rabbit, fried snake, and baked freshwater eels. Seeds, nuts, wild fruits, and vegetables are also examples of Outback foods.

Desserts

How would you like to have a food named after you? Two well-known Australian desserts are named after famous stage performers. *Pavlova,* a light meringue treat with a cream and fruit filling, is named after Anna Pavlova, a famous Russian ballet dancer. *Peach melba*—a simple dessert of peaches, berries, and whipped cream served over sponge cake—is named after an Australian opera singer, Dame Nellie Melba. Both Pavlova and Melba were famous in the early 1900s.

Looking Back on Australia

1. Two of Australia's most famous desserts are named after people. Write a newspaper article about a dish that is named after you. What is the dish called? What ingredients are in it?

2. Foods that are accepted and valued in one culture may be thought unappetizing in another. One example of this is the *bush tucker* of the Australian Aborigines. Discuss in class other examples of foods that are accepted in one culture but not in another.

3. List the foods of Australia that you would most like to try. Where can you find these foods? Which can you make?

4. In Australia, serving dishes are not placed on the table, as they often are in western cultures. Write a paragraph describing how foods are typically served in the area where you live. Are formal and informal meals served differently?

Name _____ Date _____ Class _____

About 1,500 miles off the southeast coast of Australia lie the islands of New Zealand. Although it contains several small islands, most of the country is made up of two large islands—North Island and South Island. Together these islands make up a long, skinny strip of land, which is broken near its northern end. The original settlers of the islands called them Aotearoa—Land of the Long White Cloud.

Visitors to New Zealand have many spectacular sights to choose from—steaming volcanoes, thick evergreen forests, snow-capped mountains, and sunny beaches. Both islands are very mountainous, with more than 220 mountains altogether. A mountain range in the central part of North Island has three active volcanic peaks.

The climate of New Zealand is mild and pleasant, with plenty of rain. Grass grows almost year-round on the islands, which makes it ideal grazing land for dairy and beef cattle and sheep. The weather and land are also well suited to crop farming. New Zealand farms are among the most productive in the world.

Food Traveler's Notes

Agriculture

Sheep farming is the most important element of New Zealand agriculture. More than 50 million sheep graze on the green slopes of these islands! Other kinds of livestock includes cattle, goats, and pigs. Crop farming is also important in New Zealand. Barley, wheat, corn, and oats are the largest crops, but farmers also grow apples, pears, peas, and kiwi fruit.

People and Language

New Zealanders are sometimes called "Kiwis." This nickname comes from the "kiwi," a long-beaked flightless bird that is found only in New Zealand. The fuzzy green kiwi fruit that is grown in New Zealand is also named after this unusual bird.

The original New Zealand settlers were the *Maori,* a group of people who migrated from the Polynesian islands. The Maori were joined by groups of British settlers, who started to arrive on the islands in the late 18th and early 19th centuries. Today, approximately 73 percent of the 3.5 million New Zealanders are descendants of those European settlers. Another 12 percent of New Zealand's total population are Maoris. Although both Maori and English are official languages here, almost everyone speaks English.

Dining

Because so many New Zealanders are descended from the British, New Zealand cuisine and dining patterns are very similar to those in Great Britain. Such New Zealand favorites as hot meat pies, fish and chips, and "bangers" (sausages) all come from British cuisine. Visitors to these islands can also sample traditional Maori cuisine. The Maori prepare much of their food by steaming it in an underground oven.

New Zealand cuisine relies mostly on foods that are grown or raised locally. Lamb, dairy foods, and fresh fruits and vegetables are the staple ingredients of many dishes. Seafood caught off the long New Zealand coastline is also an important food. Visitors to these islands will find oysters, lobsters, scallops, squid, salmon, and many other kinds of fish on the menu!

(Continued on next page)

New Zealand Food Briefs

Lamb

With more than 50 million sheep in New Zealand, it is not surprising that lamb is a favorite food! Lamb raised on these islands is considered to be some of the best in the world. New Zealanders often serve it as a juicy roast with garlic and rosemary, along with a tangy mint sauce. Another popular method of preparing lamb is to marinate it in a sweet, fruity mixture of prunes, apricots, brown sugar, and various spices. Visitors to New Zealand may also sample lamb cutlets, chops, stews, and even minced lamb patties!

Hangi

A *hangi* is a traditional Maori feast of foods steamed in an earth oven. The Maori prepare almost any kind of meat, fish, poultry, and vegetables this way. The first step in preparing a hangi is to dig a deep pit in the ground and heat stones over a fire. When the stones are red-hot, they are placed in the pit. Baskets of food, covered with damp cloths, are lowered into the pit on top of the stones. The Maoris then fill the hole with dirt and let the food steam for two to three hours. In traditional Maori culture, no one is allowed to walk over the pit while the food is being steamed.

ANZAC Biscuits

ANZAC biscuits are sweet cookies made of coconut, oats, sugar, flour, and butter. In both New Zealand and Australia, these cookies are associated with ANZAC Day, a public holiday honoring the Australian and New Zealand Army Corps (ANZAC). No one is certain of the history of these treats, but New Zealanders have lots of stories about them! According to one story, the ANZAC troops created the biscuits during a war, using whatever ingredients they could find. Another story is that the biscuits were created and sold to raise money for ANZAC troops during World War I. Still another version suggests that families in New Zealand and Australia baked these biscuits to send to the troops serving overseas. No matter how ANZAC biscuits were first created, these traditional cookies continue to be a New Zealand favorite!

Looking Back on New Zealand

1. In many cultures, certain foods are associated with special events in that culture's history, such as New Zealand's ANZAC biscuits. Research and write a report about other foods that are traditionally eaten on certain occasions. What is the significance of these foods?

2. When buying or preparing lamb, New Zealanders have several options to choose from: baby lamb, spring lamb, yearling, and mutton. Research and explain the differences between these kinds of lamb. Which kinds are generally considered to be the best?

3. List the foods of New Zealand that you would most like to try. Where can you find these foods? Which can you make?

4. Several foods that are popular in New Zealand come directly from British cuisine. Brainstorm with your classmates any favorite foods in your culture that come directly from another culture.

Lamb Chops with Orange Sauce

Lamb Chops with Orange Sauce

Customary	Ingredients	Metric
2 Tbsp.	Vegetable oil	30 mL
6	Shoulder lamb chops, about 1 inch (2.5 cm) thick	6
2 tsp.	Salt	10 mL
1/4 cup	Vinegar	50 mL
1 cup	Orange juice	250 mL
1/2 cup	Brown sugar	125 mL
1 Tbsp.	Lemon juice	15 mL
1/2 tsp.	Ground ginger	2 mL
1	Navel orange, thinly sliced	1

Yield: 6 servings

Directions

Pan: Large skillet; large baking dish

1. Sprinkle both sides of lamb chops with salt.

2. Heat oil in a large skillet over medium heat. Add the lamb chops and brown on both sides.

3. Place the browned chops into a baking dish in one layer.

4. Preheat oven to 350°F (180°C).

(Continued on next page)

Recipe 47 Lamb chops (continued)

5. Drain and discard oil in skillet. Add the vinegar to the empty skillet and bring to a boil. Scrape the browned bits of cooked-on lamb from the bottom and sides of the skillet, stirring them into the vinegar.

6. Remove skillet from heat. Stir in the fruit juices, brown sugar, and ginger. Pour the sauce over the lamb chops.

7. Bake, uncovered, for 30 minutes, occasionally spooning sauce from the dish over each chop to keep it moist.

8. Place lamb chops on a heated platter. Pour sauce over chops. Garnish with the orange slices before serving.

Nutrition Information: Serving size: $^1/_6$ recipe

calories: 271
total fat: 12 g
saturated fat: 3 g
cholesterol: 52 mg
sodium: 766 mg

carbohydrate: 25 g
dietary fiber: 0.6 g
sugars: 23 g
protein: 16 g

Percent Daily Value: vitamin A 1%, vitamin C 44%, calcium 4%, iron 12%

Chicken Salad with Fruit and Rice

Chicken Salad with Fruit and Rice

Customary	Ingredients	Metric
5 cups	Water	1.25 L
1 tsp.	Salt	5 mL
1¹/₂ lb.	Chicken pieces	750 g
8 tsp.	Red wine vinegar	40 mL
6 Tbsp.	Vegetable oil	90 mL
	Ground pepper (to taste)	
1¹/₂ cups	Long-grain rice	350 mL
2	Kiwi fruit	2
1	Orange	1
¹/₂ cup	Green onions, finely chopped	125 mL
3 Tbsp.	Almonds or macadamia nuts, chopped	5 mL
¹/₂ tsp.	Ground ginger	2 mL

Yield: 4 to 6 servings

Directions

Pan: Large pot; medium saucepan

1. Rinse chicken pieces and pat dry with paper towels.

2. In a large pot, bring water and salt to a boil. Add chicken pieces and cover. Simmer over low heat for about 30 minutes.

3. Remove chicken pieces and place in a colander in the sink to drain and cool.

(Continued on next page)

Recipe 48 Chicken Salad (continued)

4. Put 3 cups (750 mL) of the cooking liquid into a medium saucepan and set aside.

5. When the chicken is cool, remove the bones and skin. Cut the meat into bite-size chunks. Place in a bowl and set aside.

6. Mix vinegar, oil, pepper, and ginger. Pour 3 Tbsp. (45 mL) of this mixture over the chicken. Reserve the rest of the mixture for dressing.

7. Place the rice in a strainer and rinse with cold water. Add rice to saucepan holding cooking liquid. Bring to a boil, cover, and reduce heat to its lowest point. Cook until rice is tender, about 12 minutes.

8. Pour rice into a large bowl. Allow to cool.

9. When rice is cool, add the chicken, chopped green onions, and reserved dressing. Toss lightly.

10. Peel and cut kiwi fruit into slices; cut each slice into fourths. Peel and chop the orange. Add fruits to the salad and toss. Sprinkle chopped nuts on top.

Nutrition Information: Serving size: 1/6 recipe

calories: 513
total fat: 25 g
saturated fat: 4 g
cholesterol: 85 mg
sodium: 436 mg

carbohydrate: 37 g
dietary fiber: 3 g
sugars: 5 g
protein: 35 g

Percent Daily Value: vitamin A 7%, vitamin C 67%, calcium 6%, iron 14%

Pavlova

(Dessert of Australia and New Zealand)

Recipe 49

Touring Australia and Oceania

Pavlova
(Dessert of Australia and New Zealand)

Customary	Ingredients	Metric
3	Egg whites	3
3/4 cup	Sugar	175 mL
1/8 tsp.	Salt	0.5 mL
1 tsp.	Vanilla extract	5 mL
1 tsp.	Vinegar	5 mL
2 cups	Reduced-calorie whipped topping or whipped cream	500 mL
1 cup	Kiwi fruit slices	250 mL

Yield: 6 servings

Directions

Pan: 8-inch (20-cm) springform pan

1. Preheat oven to 350°F (180°C). Line bottom of pan with waxed paper. Line sides of pan with a strip of waxed paper extending 2 inches (5 cm) above rim.

2. Beat egg whites to soft-peak stage. Add salt and sugar, 1 Tbsp. (15 mL) at a time and continue beating until sugar is dissolved.

3. Add vanilla extract and vinegar. Beat until stiff peaks form.

4. Spread meringue evenly over bottom of prepared pan.

5. Bake at 350°F (180°C) until meringue begins to rise, about 10 to 20 minutes.

6. Reduce heat to 175°F (80°C). Bake 1 hour longer.

7. Remove meringue from oven. Let cool in pan on wire rack.

8. Remove sides from pan. Spread whipped topping over meringue. Arrange kiwi fruit slices in circular pattern over whipped topping. Slice and serve.

Nutrition Information: Serving size: 1/6 recipe

calories: 123
total fat: 1 g
saturated fat: 0 g
cholesterol: 0 mg
sodium: 79 mg

carbohydrate: 28 g
dietary fiber: 1 g
sugars: 26 g
protein: 2 g

Percent Daily Value: vitamin A 0%, vitamin C 41%, calcium 1%, iron 0%

Tip for Success

◆ If a springform pan is not available, line a baking sheet with foil. Spread meringue in an 8-inch (23-cm) circle. Bake as directed.

Teaching Global Awareness

The growing interdependence of the world's people has made taking a global perspective on many issues a necessity rather than an option.

An effective way for teachers to promote this global perspective in a foods class is to raise students' awareness of both world interdependence and the unequal distribution of the world's resources. Many students are not fully aware of how this distribution affects their food supply and food choices.

In the United States, most students select foods based mainly on what they want or like to eat rather than what they need or what is available. They eat for a variety of reasons, only one of which is hunger. They may eat because the sight or smell of a food tempts them. They may eat because food is served at a social function or simply because it's mealtime.

To gain a global perspective, students need to understand that in many parts of the world, people eat because they are hungry, eat whatever is available, and frequently do not have enough food to satisfy their hunger. In a country where many health problems are the result of eating too much or too many high-fat foods, it is difficult for many students to comprehend that there are countries where most health problems result from hunger or nutritional deficiencies.

Most students are aware of human suffering only when it is reported in the news. Hunger related to natural disasters, war, or famine is reported periodically, and these reports often trigger widespread public response. However, malnutrition and chronic hunger are pervasive, constant, and, for the most part, unreported. Hunger that occurs at a distance is easy to put out of mind. People who could not pass a hungry person in the street easily ignore the thousands who die of hunger every day. To help solve world hunger problems, students need to become more aware of the world hunger facts and of the causes and effects of unequal supply and distribution of food.

Suggested Objectives

With respect to foods and nutrition, global awareness includes awareness of the following:

◆ Local dependence on the global food supply and distribution.
◆ The unequal distribution of population, and the results of this inequality.
◆ Other factors that affect global and local food supplies and food choices.
◆ Causes of food shortages and famine.
◆ Global patterns of distribution that lead to dietary deficiency and dietary excess.

Global awareness will encourage and enable students to:

◆ Identify public policy issues that affect global nutrition and health.
◆ Understand the role of the individual in the public policy process.
◆ Propose and discuss solutions to the world food crisis.
◆ Take actions to help address world hunger.

Internet Disclaimer: The Internet listings that follow are a source for extended information on the topics in this book. We have made every effort to recommend sites that are informative and accurate. However, these sites are not under the control of Glencoe/McGraw-Hill, and, therefore, Glencoe/McGraw-Hill makes no representation concerning the content of these sites. We strongly encourage teachers to preview Internet sites before students use them. Many sites may eventually contain "hot links" to other sites that could lead to exposure to inappropriate material. Internet sites are sometimes "under construction" and may not always be available. Sites may also move or have been discontinued completely by the time you or your students attempt to access them.

Suggested References for Teaching Global Awareness

Books

Cohen, Marc J., ed., *What Governments Can Do: Hunger 1997*. Silver Spring, Md.: Bread for the World, 1996.

Harley, Richard M. *Breakthroughs on Hunger: A Journalist's Encounter with Global Change*. Washington, D.C.: Smithsonian, 1990.

Howard, Tracy A., and Sage A. Howard. *Kids Ending Hunger: What Can We Do?* Kansas City, Mo.: Andrews & McMeel, 1992.

The Hunger Project. Ending Hunger: An Idea Whose Time Has Come. New York: Praeger, 1985.

Articles

Combs, Jr., Gerald F., Welch, Ross M., et al. "Fighting Hidden Hunger." *World & I,* April 1998, p. 174.

de Souza, Herbert, and Edgar Morin. "A Country in Arms Against Hunger." *UNESCO Courier,* March 1995, pp. 26-29.

"A Food Crisis-Or a Blip?" *World Press Review,* February 1996, p. 34.

MacKenzie, Debora. "China Crisis." *New Scientist,* April 25, 1998, p. 16.

Poppendieck, Janet. "Want Amid Plenty: From Hunger to Inequality." *Monthly Labor Review,* July/August 1998, p. 125.

Speth, James G. "Food First." *Choices: The Human Development Magazine,* June 1994, pp. 24-26.

Van Luyn, Floris-Jan. "A Hunger for More Than Rice." *World Press Review,* March 1996, pp. 38-39.

"Winning the Food Race." *Population Reports,* December 1997, pp. 1-2.

Organizations

American Forum for Global Education
120 Wall Street, Suite 2600
New York, NY 10038
http://www.globaled.org/
Email: globed120@aol.com

Works with educators at all levels to enhance global perspectives education. Offers instructional materials, consulting services, professional development programs, and study tours for educators.

American Friends Service Committee
1501 Cherry Street
Philadelphia, PA 19102
http://www.afsc.org/
Email: afsinfo@afsc.org

Work includes development and refugee relief, peace education, and community organizing. Offers booklets, program literature, and audiovisual materials.

(Continued on next page)

Bread for the World
1100 Wayne Avenue, Suite 1000
Silver Spring, MD 20910
http://www.bread.org
Offers research and education on polices related to hunger and development. Produces various newsletters, reports, and videos.

Care
151 Ellis Street, NE
Atlanta, GA 30303
http://www.care.org
Email: info@care.org
Produces printed materials and audiovisual resources on food production, health care, and other development issues.

Church World Service
28606 Phillips Street
P.O. Box 968
Elkhart, IN 46515
http://www.ncccusa.org/cws/mainone.html
Email: cws@ncccusa.org
Maintains a film and video lending library of materials on hunger and development issues. Sponsors Crop Walks.

The Hunger Project
15 East Twenty-sixth Street
New York, NY 10010
http://www.cgv.org/thp
Email: info@thp.org
Conducts educational courses and workshops aimed at eliminating world hunger. Publishes A Shift in the Wind newspaper, African Farmer magazine, and other publications.

Institute for Food and Development Policy (Food First)
398 Sixtieth Street
Oakland, CA 94618
http://www.foodfirst.org/index.html
Email: foodfirst@igc.apc.org
Focuses on social and economic causes of world hunger. Produces various publications and videos.

(Continued on next page)

◆ **A Global Foods Tour** **149**

National Student Campaign Against Hunger and Homelessness
11965 Venice Boulevard, Suite 408
Los Angeles, CA 90066

http://www.pirg.org/nscahh

Email: nscah@aol.com

Works with students across the country to end hunger and homelessness through education, service, and action. Publishes newsletters and manuals for students establishing programs to combat poverty.

Oxfam America
26 West Street
Boston, MA 02111

http://www.oxfamamerica.org

Email: info@oxfamamerica.org

Provides education on the root causes of hunger and funding assistance to self-help community development projects. Publishes Viewpoint newsletter.

Save the Children Federation
54 Wilton Road
Westport, CT 06881

http://www.savethechildren.org

Assists children, families, and communities abroad and in the U.S. to achieve social and economic stability. Publishes Impact Magazine and Save the Children Reports.

U.S. Committee for the United Nations Children's Fund
333 East Thirty-eighth Street
New York, NY 10016

http://www.unicefusa.org

Email: webmaster@unicefusa.org

Promotes the survival, protection, and development of children worldwide through fundraising, advocacy, and education. Offers teaching and program aids, including videos.

U.S. National Committee for World Food Day
1001 Twenty-second Street, NW
Washington, DC 20437

Coordinates U.S. activities for World Food Day on October 16. Publishes materials for observing the day.

Activities and Projects for Teaching Global Awareness

Supermarket Field Trip. Arrange to take students to visit a large supermarket. Ask the produce manager to identify the origins of several imported produce items. Next organize students into groups and assign each group an aisle. Have groups list foods from other countries. After the trip, have students imagine they live in another country and identify the foods they could eat if they were dependent only on locally produced food. Discuss the role of world trade, transportation, refrigeration, and electricity in food supply and food choices.

Global Population Handout. Reproduce and distribute **Global Awareness Handout 1, "World Population Growth"** (page 152). Have students complete the line graph as directed (1000-1700: 700; 1700-1850: 150; 1850-1956: 106; 1956-1994: 38; 1994-2100: 106). Ask students to predict whether the time it will take for the population at 2100 to double will be greater or less than the time noted by the last line on the chart. Discuss population growth as a factor that affects world resources, including the food supply.

Agriculture Research. Have students research farming methods in this country that have increased food yields. How do they compare with food production methods in countries where food is often in short supply? Could the technological advances in the U.S. be put to use in these countries? Why or why not?

Distribution of Resources Handout. Reproduce and distribute **Global Awareness Handout 2, "Distribution of Resources"** (page 153). Initiate a class discussion based on the questions at the end of the article. (Possible answers: 1. Children depend on others to care for them. Children and women are more likely to be impoverished because of a variety of social factors. 2. Without arable land, crops cannot be produced. 3. Stockpiled food is useless if it spoils or can't be transported to those who need it. 4. Overconsumption in one part of the world means less to go around in other places. 5. Avoid overconsumption; support organizations that combat world hunger; make others aware of the problem.)

Types of Hunger Handout. Reproduce and distribute **Global Awareness Handout 3, "Types of Hunger"** (pages 154). After students have read the handout, discuss the differences between the terms *seasonal hunger, chronic undernutrition, malnutrition,* and *famine.* Ask students the following questions: Which gets the most media attention? (famine) Which is least often reported? (chronic undernutrition) Which is a problem even in parts of the world where people have plenty to eat? (malnutrition) Have students use a world map to show two areas where famine has occurred in the last decade (North Korea and Sudan) and two other areas where chronic undernutrition is a widespread problem. (Sub-Saharan Africa and South Asia)

Reasons for Eating Project. Reproduce and distribute **GA Project 1, "Reasons for Eating-A Global Perspective"** (pages 155-56). To help students better understand reasons for eating and influences on reasons, have them complete the project as directed.

Food Choices Project. Reproduce and distribute **GA Project 2, "What Did You Eat? What Would You Eat?"** (pages 157-58). To broaden students' views of food consumption patterns, have them complete the project as directed.

Food Supply Project. Reproduce and distribute **GA Project 3, "Factors Affecting the Food Supply"** (page 159). To help students analyze how given factors affect the food supply in a specific country, have them complete the project as directed.

Personal Action Project. Reproduce and distribute **GA Project 4, "Two Problems, One Solution"** (page 160). To help students explore a strategy for avoiding dietary excess and for feeding the hungry, have them complete the project as directed.

Global Awareness Handout 1

World Population Growth

World population growth since the year 1000 is shown in the table below. The table also includes predictions of future world population growth through the year 2150. This table is based on information from the U.S. Bureau of the Census: International Data Base; Historical Estimates of World Population and from the Population Information Network (POPIN) of the United Nations Population Division, Department for Economic and Social Information and Policy Analysis.

Many organizations and individuals calculate past, present, and future world population.

The conclusions of one group may not agree exactly with the conclusions of another group. Every group's final figures are influenced by the data and methods used to analyze and to interpret the data.

Analyze Data

As you can see, the rate of population growth has not remained stable. Complete the line graph on this page to illustrate the changes in the number of years required for the world population to double. For each span of years listed, draw a horizontal line of the correct length. The first line has been drawn for you.

World Population

Year	Population in billions
1000	0.30
1700	0.67
1850	1.40
1956	2.80
1994	5.60
2100	11.19
2150	11.54

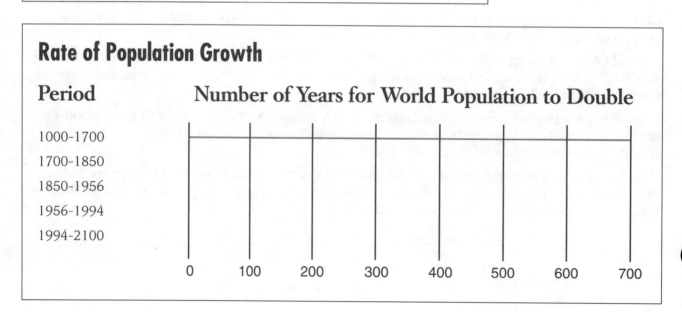

Rate of Population Growth

Period	Number of Years for World Population to Double
1000–1700	
1700–1850	
1850–1956	
1956–1994	
1994–2100	

0   100   200   300   400   500   600   700

Global Awareness Handout 2

Distribution of Resources

Consider these facts:

◆ In 1995, more than enough food was produced to give every person in the world a minimum of 2,350 calories per day.

◆ In 1996, the estimated number of hungry people in the world was 841 million—well over triple the population of the United States. A high percentage of those who go hungry are children under age 18. Women represent the next largest group.

If more than enough food is being produced worldwide to give everyone adequate nutrition, why are so many people going hungry? The answer to this question can be found by examining the distribution of the world's people and resources.

Neither resources nor people are distributed evenly over the globe. In the mid-1990s, more than 70 percent of the world's people lived in developing countries—approximately 120 countries in Africa, Asia, and Latin America. These countries have economies based primarily on agriculture. There are few industries.

While the developing countries are home to a large percentage of the world population, they do not have a large percentage of the world's resources. More than half of the people in the developing world live in extreme poverty. Local resources are often insufficient to feed the local population. In Kenya, for example, only 4 percent of the country's area is *arable land*—land that can be used to grow crops.

In addition to their lack of arable land, facilities for storage, preservation, and transportation of food also tend to be in short supply in developing countries. The net result of the high levels of population and low levels of resources in the developing world is hunger. On average, people in developing countries consume fewer calories per day than is considered necessary for maintaining good health.

In contrast, the United States and the other industrialized countries that make up the developed world support only about 30 percent of the world's population. Arable land in the United States is calculated at about 21 percent of the total area.

Hunger is certainly not unknown in the United States. According to the U.S. Bureau of the Census, in 1995, about 13.8 percent of people in the United States lived in poverty. Still, on average, people living in the United States consume over 3,000 calories each day—much more than they need for maintaining good health.

For Thought and Discussion

1. Why, do you suppose, are so many of the hungry people in the world children?

2. Why is the percentage of arable land in a particular country significant?

3. Why does a lack of facilities for storage, preservation, and transportation of food result in hunger?

4. What effect does overconsumption in affluent countries have on world resources?

5. What can people in the United States and other affluent nations do to help solve the problem of world hunger?

Global Awareness Handout 3

Types of Hunger

Many people are concerned about world hunger and are seeking a solution. Actually, world hunger is more than one problem. There are different types of hunger, and each has its own circumstances. To help find solutions to world hunger, you must first understand the types of hunger that occur.

Seasonal Undernutrition

In some areas, food from the last harvest runs out before food from the current planting is ready to eat. People often go hungry for weeks, sometimes months, waiting for the new crops to mature and be ready to harvest. This type of hunger, known as *seasonal undernutrition,* frequently happens in many African countries, where the month of May is often referred to as "the month children wait for food."

Chronic Undernutrition

Seasonal undernutrition is cyclical. However, when an individual consumes fewer calories and nutrients than his or her body needs over a long period of time, the condition is called *chronic undernutrition.* Chronic undernutrition lowers a person's ability to work productively, to think clearly, and to resist diseases. Common diseases that are easily handled by well-nourished people can be fatal to the chronically undernourished.

Statistics from the Subcommittee on Nutrition of the United Nations show that in 1990, 184 million children suffered from seasonal or chronic undernutrition. Some researchers think the number may be greater. In areas where hunger is chronic, the resulting health problems are accepted as the normal state of life. The condition is rarely reported because it is not unusual.

Malnutrition

Malnutrition is a state of ill health related to nutrition. Malnutrition can be categorized by its cause. People who are ill because they regularly do not get the proper amount of food or the right kinds of food have *primary malnutrition.* People who have poor health because their body cannot use the nutrients from the foods they eat have *secondary malnutrition.*

Physicians further categorize types of malnutrition by identifying the nutrient or nutrients that are missing. For example, malnutrition caused by insufficient intake of vitamins results in specific vitamin deficiencies. Statistics from the 1980s show that about 14 million children under 5 years of age suffered from vitamin A deficiency. It is estimated that nearly 250,000 children become blind every year as a result of long-term vitamin A deficiency.

Malnutrition can also occur without hunger if a person eats too much of the wrong foods. Too much vitamin A, for instance, can cause problems that range from skin rashes to liver failure and death. Taking in too many calories and too much fat and cholesterol can contribute to obesity and heart disease.

Famine

Famine is a widespread food shortage that continues for months or years and causes hunger and death. Famine can occur when bad weather, natural disasters, political upheaval, or war disrupts the food supply. Those affected are often already among the chronically undernourished. Statistics for 1992 from the World Hunger Program at Brown University show that between 15 and 35 million people were at risk for famine. Famine is a continuing threat for many developing countries.

During a famine, food may be available within the stricken area, but large segments of the population may not have access to it. High prices may deny food to all but the wealthy. Delivery and distribution systems may break down, preventing food from reaching people who need it.

Although only 10 percent of the world's hunger is due to famine, it is the most commonly reported type of hunger.

For Thought and Discussion

1. Which type of hunger gets the most media attention?
2. Which type of hunger is least often reported?
3. Which type of hunger is a problem even in parts of the world where people have plenty to eat?
4. Through library or Internet research, locate two parts of the world where famine has occurred in the last two decades.

Global Awareness Project 1

Reasons for Eating—A Global Perspective

The majority of people living in the United States have some choice about when and what they eat. For many people, however, including some who live in the United States, eating is a matter of survival. Food choices are limited, and meal time is whenever food is available. Completing this activity will help you better understand this contrast in eating patterns.

Purpose

To examine reasons for eating in the United States; to speculate about reasons for eating in places where food is scarce; and to contrast the two.

Resources

◆ Books (including textbooks) and periodicals that focus on food distribution and eating patterns

◆ Internet and other information sources that focus on food distribution and eating patterns

◆ Organizations that provide information on world hunger

Materials

◆ Reasons for Eating-A Global Perspective Survey provided on page 156.

Procedure

1. Interview ten people of varying ages and backgrounds. Survey their reasons for eating by asking them the questions listed on the survey form. Tally their responses in the appropriate column next to each question on the form.

2. Analyze the results of the survey. Which three reasons were most commonly given? How many people said they ate just to survive?

3. Conduct research about a low-income population in a country where chronic hunger exists. (You might choose to research a country that has been in the news. India, Sub-Saharan Africa, and parts of Asia have long histories of hunger.) What is a typical day like for people in a society where chronic hunger exists?

4. How might a person in the society you researched respond to your survey? Respond to the survey as you think that person would. Record your answers separately from the other responses.

5. Write a short paper summarizing your findings and conclusions. Explain how people's reasons for eating might differ in an affluent society as compared to an impoverished society.

(Continued on next page)

Global Awareness Project 1 (continued)

Reasons for Eating—A Global Perspective Survey

Questions to Ask	Yes	No
Have you ever eaten only because you're tempted by a food you can't resist?		
Have you ever eaten only because you're bored?		
Have you ever eaten only because food is a part of a certain social occasion?		
Have you ever eaten only because it was meal-time?		
Have you ever eaten only for the pleasure of eating?		
Have you ever eaten only to comfort yourself when you're sad or upset?		
Have you ever eaten only to survive?		

Global Awareness Project 2

What Did You Eat? What Would You Eat?

In any country, the economic status of the people has a major influence on the foods eaten. The affluent (those who are well-off, or prosperous) have a greater choice of foods than do the impoverished. The cuisine most people associate with a country is likely to be that of the upper and middle classes. The food consumed by the poorest people, who are sometimes the majority of a country's population may be very different.

Purpose

To compare food choices and consumption in the United States with both the affluent and impoverished classes of another country.

Resources

◆ Books (including textbooks) and periodicals that focus on food distribution and eating patterns

◆ Internet and other information sources that focus on food distribution and eating patterns

◆ Menus from ethnic restaurants or recipes from ethnic cookbooks

Materials

◆ Three copies of the What Did You Eat? What Would You Eat? Data Chart provided on page 158.

Procedure

1. Write "United States" at the top of one copy of the chart. Choose a day in the last week for which you can recall everything that you ate. Write down what you ate and the amount of food eaten for breakfast, lunch, dinner, and snacks.

2. Choose a country to research. Be sure its population includes (or did at one time) both affluent people and impoverished people.

3. Research the meal patterns and typical food choices of affluent people in the country you have chosen.

4. Write the name of the country and "Affluent" on a second copy of the chart. Fill in the columns with foods you might eat in a day if you lived with an affluent family in that country. (Meal patterns may be different from your own.)

5. Research the meal patterns and typical food choices of impoverished people in the country you have chosen.

6. Write the name of the country and "Impoverished" on a third copy of the chart. Fill in the columns with foods you might eat in a day if you lived with an impoverished family in that country. (Meal patterns may be different from your own and from the affluent people of the country.)

7. Write a brief paper comparing how your present eating habits and expectations would change if you first became part of an affluent and then an impoverished family from the country you researched.

(Continued on next page)

Global Awareness GA Project 2 (continued)

What Did You Eat? What Would You Eat? Data Chart		
Country: _____		
Meal	*Food Eaten*	*Amount Eaten*
Breakfast		
Lunch		
Dinner		
Snacks		
Other Meals (explain)		

Global Awareness Project 3

Factors Affecting the Food Supply

The food supply in a given area is affected by many factors. Sometimes one or more of these factors causes food to be scarce. As a result, people go hungry. Finding a solution to world hunger begins with an understanding of the factors that cause it.

Purpose

To analyze how given factors affect the food supply in a specific country.

Resources

◆ Books (including textbooks) and periodicals that focus on food production and distribution

◆ Internet and other information sources that focus on food production and distribution

◆ Atlas

◆ Organizations that provide information on world hunger

Materials

◆ Materials (such as poster board and markers) for making visual aids

◆ Computer with graphing and chart-making software

Procedure

1. Form a team with your classmates, as instructed by your teacher.

2. Choose a country for your team to research or obtain an assigned country from your teacher.

3. Assign each team member to learn about the current status of one or more of the following factors as it relates to the food supply of the country you are studying:

◆ geography

◆ climate

◆ economics

◆ transportation systems

◆ farming methods

◆ fuel supply

◆ population density

◆ political situation

◆ natural disasters

4. Research your assigned factor. Write a brief summary of how that factor does affect or might affect the food supply.

5. Share your findings with the other members of your team. As a team, decide which three factors have the greatest effect on or greatest potential to affect the food supply in your assigned country.

6. As a team, prepare and present a brief oral report summarizing your team's findings and conclusions. Use at least one visual aid, such as a graph or chart, in your presentation.

Global Awareness Project 4

Two Problems, One Solution

The Dietary Guidelines for Americans encourage people to balance the amounts and kinds of foods they eat with their levels of physical activity and to choose foods low in fat and moderate in sodium and sugar. Yet many people in the United States snack from habit rather than from a need for energy. Also, the most popular snacks are high in fat, sodium, and sugar. The main food-related problem for many people in the United States is dietary excess. In some areas of the world, dietary deficiency is the main food-related problem. Getting enough food to meet minimum energy needs is a daily challenge for the hungry.

Purpose

To explore a strategy for avoiding dietary excess and helping to feed the hungry.

Resources

◆ Books (including textbooks) and periodicals that focus on food distribution and eating patterns

◆ Internet and other information sources that focus on food distribution and eating patterns

◆ Organizations that provide information on world hunger

◆ Restaurants and food stores

Materials

◆ Computer and word processing software or drawing paper and marking pens

Procedure

1. Working in groups, brainstorm to make a list of popular snack foods or beverages that contain large amounts of fat, sodium, or sugar.

2. Assign each group member one or more items on the list. Find prices for these foods or beverages in food stores or restaurants. How much, for example, does a hot fudge sundae cost? A chocolate bar? A large bag of potato chips?

3. Call or write several organizations that work to combat world hunger. (Your teacher can help you find such organizations.) Find out how much food a given amount of money will buy for hungry people in developing countries. Figures will vary depending on the country and the organization. Some organizations will have figures about the number of persons that can be fed; others may be able to tell you the number of meals served or the amount of beans or grain that can be purchased.

4. Calculate how much help can be provided for the price of each food or beverage you listed in Step 1. For example, you may find that the price of a large chocolate bar will feed two children for a day.

5. As a class, compile your results. Create and distribute flyers to make the information available to your family, friends, and students in your school. Your flyer should ask, in some form, the question "Would you be willing to give up a snack now in order to provide food for the hungry?" On your flyers, include the names and addresses of organizations that help feed the hungry.